BILL BRADLEY is a graduate of Princeton University, where he received honors in American history, and Oxford University, where he studied as a Rhodes scholar. He played professional basketball for ten years with the New York Knicks. The people of New Jersey elected him to the U.S. Senate in 1978. He serves on the Finance Committee and on the Energy and Natural Resources Committee, and he has chaired two task forces on economic growth for the Senate Democratic Caucus. He lives in northern New Jersey with his wife, Ernestine, and daughter, Theresa Anne.

Most Pocket Books are available at special quantity discounts for bulk purchases for sales promotions, premiums or fund raising. Special books or book excerpts can also be created to fit specific needs.

For details write the office of the Vice President of Special Markets, Pocket Books, 1230 Avenue of the Americas, New York, New York 10020.

THE FAIR TAX

By Senator Bill Bradley

PUBLISHED BY POCKET BOOKS NEW YORK

336.24
B728

Another *Original* publication of POCKET BOOKS

POCKET BOOKS, a division of Simon & Schuster, Inc.
1230 Avenue of the Americas, New York, N.Y. 10020

Copyright © 1984 by Fair Tax Foundation
Cover photograph copyright © 1984 by Ronald L. Freenan

All rights reserved, including the right to reproduce
this book or portions thereof in any form whatsoever.
For information address Pocket Books, 1230 Avenue
of the Americas, New York, N.Y. 10020

ISBN: 0-671-46544-9

First Pocket Books printing July, 1984

10 9 8 7 6 5 4 3 2 1

POCKET and colophon are registered trademarks
of Simon & Schuster, Inc.

Printed in the U.S.A.

ACKNOWLEDGMENTS

For ten years I have believed America needs and deserves a new tax system. This book is written in hopes of rallying support for the Fair Tax.

Many people have given generous support and encouragement. In particular, I want to thank Jim Wetzler and Randy Weiss of the Joint Tax Committee for their invaluable assistance in drafting the bill. Doug Drysdale, Tom Troyer, Bob Klayman, Stanley Surry, Joe Pechman, Dan Halperin, Don Lubick, Jerry Kurtz, Paul McDaniel, Emil Sunly and Dale Collinson were instrumental in the inception and the refinement of the Fair Tax. Members of the New Jersey Bar Association gave valuable advice, as did Mark Gasarch and Peter Baumbusch. David Bradford provided insightful criticism, while the Tax Section of the New York State Bar Association did yeoman service in reviewing and commenting on the bill's initial draft.

ACKNOWLEDGMENTS

Roger Mentz, Don Alexander and Ann O'Connell were particularly helpful in this regard.

My special thanks go to Dick Gephardt, my co-sponsor and friend. He cares about America and what a fair-tax system can mean for all of us. He helped shape the bill and now carries the argument effectively in the House of Representatives where he is assisted ably by Jim Jaffee, his Administrative Assistant. Finally, I want to express my deep appreciation to Dick Lerner and Doyle McManus who helped smooth the prose; to Joe Minarek, whose unstinting contribution of time, effort, and ideas have been central to this project since the beginning, and, most important, to Gina DesPres, my legislative counsel, whose intelligence guided the development of the bill and who has lived this project for four years with intensity and commitment.

CONTENTS

THE
FAIR
TAX

INTRODUCTION

"Taxes," said the great Supreme Court Justice Oliver Wendell Holmes, Jr., "are the price we pay for a civilized society."

Until recently, most Americans felt that the price we paid for the benefits of our society was pretty reasonable. Paying taxes was never a happy task, but the vast majority of us paid willingly and honestly, confident that our neighbors were paying their fair shares as well.

But our income tax isn't working that way any more. It's unfair. It's overly complex. It's distorting investment decisions, encouraging people to put money into schemes to reduce their tax bills instead of enterprises to create jobs and to help our economy grow.

And the American people know it. Polls consistently show that a majority of Americans believes the present tax system is fundamentally inequitable. They believe that middle-income and lower-income people pay more in taxes than the wealthy. They resent the thick book of tax instructions that arrives at tax time each year. And most of all they want lower tax rates for everybody.

There's no mystery why people feel this way. A few familiar examples:

—According to the Brookings Institution, in 1981, families who reported income of more than $1 million paid an effective tax rate of only 17.7 percent and they did it legally, through the use of "loopholes."

—In 1984, a family with $29,000 in income may pay $3,560 in federal income taxes. Another family with the same income, using a few common loopholes, may pay $2,830. A third family—still with the same $29,000 income—may pay nothing at all.

—The current federal tax code is more than 2,000 pages long, almost twice as long as most King James versions of the Bible. To interpret its complex and often confusing provisions, we employ almost 80,000 tax lawyers and accountants, more than twice the number of directory assistance operators in the United States.

—At a time when our economy faces tough challenges from foreign competition, the tax system has created an entire industry—the tax shelter industry— devoted to the inefficient use of investment capital. That industry employs thousands of talented people whose only job is to find schemes that will reduce the investors' tax bills, not to build the new industries our nation needs to remain the number one economic power in the world.

—As loopholes and shelters have sprung up, the tradition of "voluntary compliance" has weakened. The IRS estimates that since 1973, unreported income has ballooned from approximately $94 billion to almost

$250 billion in 1981. This translates into an increase in lost tax revenues from approximately $29 billion in 1973 to almost $82 billion in 1981. By now that figure is approaching $100 billion. That means that the tax system is cheating the vast majority who do pay all their taxes—and the majority knows it. "I sometimes think I'm the only one in the neighborhood paying his taxes without a fancy tax gimmick," a New Jersey engineer complained to me. He's not alone. Financial author Adam Smith, who knows the practices of investors as well as anyone, wrote recently that he sometimes feels like "the last honest taxpayer in America."

In other words, our loss of confidence in the tax system is well-founded. And just as we have lost confidence in the tax system, we have also lost faith in our government as a whole—in its ability to respond to our needs and to help us solve our problems.

It is a vicious cycle. The unfairness of the tax laws makes us doubt whether government is still capable of overseeing the way society's burdens are distributed. The less confidence we have in government, the less willing we are to pay taxes to support it. The more we try to avoid paying taxes—the more time we all devote to finding the loopholes that will reduce each of our individual tax bills—the less equitable the system appears. The less equitable the tax system and the greater the difference in taxes paid on similar incomes, the less faith there is in government and the weaker become the bonds of our American community.

I believe there is a solution—a way to restore integrity to the tax system and, by so doing, to begin restoring confidence in government. It's called the Fair Tax.

The Fair Tax, which is now before Congress, would lower the tax rates of all Americans and would eliminate the special interest tax provisions that reward the few at the expense of higher rates for the many. The tax revenues gained from abolishing those loopholes would make it possible for everyone's tax rates to be reduced. And that would encourage the work and investment we need for long-term economic growth.

The Fair Tax would eliminate many of the itemized deductions taxpayers now use (but not the deductions for home mortgage interest, charitable contributions, or state and local income and property taxes, among others). In return, it would lower almost everyone's tax rate, and replace the present rate structure with a simplified one. Individuals would pay one of three tax rates—14, 26, or 30 percent. Four out of five taxpayers would pay the low rate of 14 percent. About 70 percent of the taxpayers would be paying less tax; 30 percent, more tax.

And the Fair Tax would simplify the tax law so that taxpayers would know in advance how much in taxes they should pay—and could be sure that their neighbors in similar circumstances would pay roughly the same amounts.

Not everyone supports that kind of sweeping tax reform, no matter how clear its advantages are. The special interests that benefit from tailor-made tax loopholes are hoping the idea will simply die.

But it is time to assert the general interest—the interest of all Americans in having a government they can believe in—over the narrow interests that too often seem to have seized control of our political life. A tax system that is equitable, understandable, and efficient is not a Democratic idea or a Republican idea. It is a national idea that should prompt all of us to look beyond individual, short-term profits—our hope of finding one more new deduction on this year's tax return—toward our long-run common interests.

That is an issue bigger than any question of loopholes, bigger even than the challenge of rebuilding a reasonable tax system. It's a question of taking a first step toward making government worthy of our confidence again.

That's what the Fair Tax is all about.

that was accidentally destroyed in the trash compactor.
—A medical deduction for your 12-year-old son's expensive dental braces that were not covered by your insurance.

And remember how you tried to decide whether you should use the tax tables to figure out your state sales tax deduction or whether it was worth going back over all those 1983 department store receipts?

As you went through that process. maybe you wondered why it was all necessary, and whether there wasn't a simpler way to pay taxes. For an example of real complexity, take the "income averaging" provision. It is supposed to let taxpayers smooth out bulges in their income from year to year so that they can avoid sharp changes in their tax liability. Suppose you have been earning about $30,000 a year for several years—and this year you win $100,000 in a lottery. Suddenly, you would have to pay much higher taxes than you paid in previous years. By using the income averaging provision, you could spread out your gain— and your taxes—over a four-year period. But if nobody told you about this, you'd never know it by the language in the Internal Revenue Code:

Sec. 1302. Definition of Averageable Income; Related Definitions

(a) Average Income.—

(1) In general.—For purposes of this part, the term "averageable income" means the amount by which taxable income for the computation year (reduced as provided in paragraph (2)) exceeds 120 percent of average base period income.

(2) Reduction.—The taxable income for the computation year shall be reduced by—

(A) The amount (if any) to which section 72(m)(5) applies, and

(B) The amounts included in the income of a beneficiary of a trust under section 667(a)

(b) Average Base Period Income.—For purposes of this part—

(1) In general.—The term "average base period income" means one-fourth of the sum of the base period incomes for the base period.

No wonder less than one third of those taxpayers eligible for income averaging claim it.

The two-earner or "marriage penalty" deduction is another good example of this problem. Under present law, couples filing a joint return are allowed a deduction in computing adjusted gross income equal to 10 percent of the lower earning spouse's *qualified income*. The maximum allowable deduction is $3,000. What, you may be wondering, is qualified income?

Assuming you could find the right Code section, the definition might well strike you as less than enlightening:

Qualified Earned Income Defined.—

(1) In general.—For purposes of this section, the term "qualified earned income" means an amount equal to the excess of—

(A) the earned income of the spouse for the taxable year, over

    (B) an amount equal to the sum of the deductions described in paragraphs (1), (2), (7), (10) and (15) of section 62 to the extent such deductions are properly allowable to or chargeable against earned income described in subparagraph (A).

The amount of qualified earned income shall be determined without regard to any community property laws.

(2) Earned Income.—For purposes of paragraph (1), the term "earned income" means income within the meaning of section 911(d)(2), or 401(c)(2)(C), except that—

    (A) such term shall not include any amount—

    (i) not includible in gross income,

    (ii) received as a pension or annuity,

    (iii) paid or distributed out of an individual retirement plan (within the meaning of section 7701(a)(37),

    (iv) received as deferred compensation, or

    (v) received for services performed by an individual in the employ of his spouse (within the meaning of section 3121(b)(3)(A), and

    (B) section 911(d)(2)(B) shall be applied without regard to the phrase "not in excess of 30 percent of his share of net profits of such trade or business."

Mind boggling, isn't it? Especially considering that this provision was intended to help Mr. and Mrs.

Working American who have long been shouldering a heavier tax burden than their single counterparts. Notwithstanding all the hoopla that accompanied the enactment of this provision, many couples eligible for the deduction aren't claiming it. Either they don't know it's there, or it's too complicated for them to figure out. I don't blame them.

The irony is that there's a much simpler way of providing two-earner couples their richly deserved relief from the marriage penalty: simplify and lower the rate structure. That way the relief is built into the system. Everyone who's eligible gets it and there's no need for complex computations.

Once a loophole gets into law it takes an explosion to get it out. The medical expense deduction, for example, was originally intended to compensate the taxpayer only for extraordinary costs. Medical expenses above 3 percent of a taxpayer's income were deductible. It was a way for the government to help pay for catastrophic health costs. But after a period of high inflation in which medical costs rose about one-third faster than other costs, a threshold of 3 percent (raised to 5 percent in 1982) of adjusted gross income was reached even for routine medical services. So now we have the income tax compensating nearly 22 million taxpapers in 1982 for, in many cases, relatively ordinary levels of medical services. A higher floor would allow lower tax rates for everyone while at the same time continuing to provide relief for those taxpayers whose medical costs are truly extraordinary. To change the floor leads to charges of cutting health care for the needy, but the most needy generally don't owe any income tax, and even when they do pay a few dollars they don't have enough deductions to itemize. It would be much better for the lower-income persons to have a health insurance system that gives them assured care and a tax system that gives them low rates.

The effect of the existing complexity is much more than increased confusion at tax time, says former IRS Commissioner Roscoe Egger:

> "There generally is a tradeoff in the tax law between equity and simplicity. That is, the more equitable we try to be in measuring ability to pay tax, the more complex the rules become. . . . Although no one such provision can be said to overburden the tax system, in total they do. When for example a tax credit is enacted to encourage or reward those who insulate their homes, which may benefit a few million taxpayers, the forms and instructions are complicated for all 100 million taxpayers. The overall effect is to render the tax system unintelligible for far too many taxpayers."

The Code's complexity not only makes it difficult for taxpayers to figure out the Code and the instructions—the courts have trouble too. Remember those 8,500 cases before the Court of Appeals. And the result is a set of laws that appears to be quite simply capricious.

On the medical deduction, for example, *The New York Times* on August 3, 1982, carried the following story:

NO ON TATTOOS

Hair removal? Yes. Wigs? Maybe. Tattoos? No. Pierced ears? No.

The Internal Revenue Service recently decided to let taxpayers write off expenses for hair implants and hair removal, but has taken a firm

stand against write-offs for tattoos and ear piercing.

Wigs, when essential for mental stability, have
been deductible since 1962.

"Tattoos and ear piercing are not medical expenses and are not tax deductible," said Roderic
Young, a spokesman for the IRS.

But times are changing. The agency took a
more sympathetic view of hair problems, revers-
ing its earlier refusal to accept hair removal by
electrolysis as a medical procedure warranting
tax relief. It also specifically allowed expenses
for hair implants by plastic surgeons.

Or how about the provision in the Code that says
you can deduct a casualty loss only if it's caused by
fire, storm, shipwreck, theft, or another sudden, unusual, unexpected, or accidental force?

When a severe four-month drought killed their roll-
ing lawn and handsome shrubs, John and Betty David-
son estimated that the value of their house dropped
$2,000 and claimed a "casualty loss" of that amount in
their tax return. Although the IRS denied the claim,
the Davidsons won a judgment in the Tax Court.

The Davidsons were lucky. Mike and Sue Warren
had a different experience when a lethal yellowing
disease wiped out all 22 palm trees surrounding their
Miami Beach house. The IRS said the Warrens could
not deduct the loss on their income tax, and this time
the Tax Court agreed—declaring that "disease"
doesn't qualify for a casualty loss even if it's relatively
sudden.

Confusing? Look at one more example.

Peter and Jean Douglas had a wonderful black oak
tree—100 years old and 80 feet high—next to their
home in Virginia. After wood borers killed its bark, the

Douglases claimed a $15,000 loss on their income tax. The IRS said no, and the Douglases went to court.

The Tax Court ruled that, although this kind of thing wouldn't normally qualify, the fact that the borers had disposed of the tree in a single summer made the loss "sudden and unexpected" and hence deductible.

With equally ambiguous and convoluted language throughout the Code and highly complex tax forms, you probably haven't been doing your own tax returns these past few years.

About 41 percent of all taxpayers had their returns prepared by lawyers, accountants, and other tax professionals in 1981 (the latest year of complete data). Because only about 33 percent of all taxpayers itemized their deductions, that means that at least some taxpayers were so intimidated by the complexity that they hired a preparer to claim the standard deduction.

Many other taxpayers now use such assistance on a year-round basis. This is not just to ease the considerable burden of record-keeping, though that is what motivates many people. It is also for "tax planning"—the careful orchestration of a person's business and personal actions to minimize his tax bill. *Want to go on a vacation?* If you listen to your tax adviser you won't go to Florida where your brother lives. You'll go to Bermuda where the state bar is holding its convention. Then you can deduct your expenses. *Need to put your child in a day care center?* Be careful. The neighborhood center might not be an IRS-approved center. You might have to drive her all the way downtown to a new corporate day care center. *Unsure about a leg operation?* Have it now because this year you've already spent 5 percent of your income on health care and next year you probably won't be able to deduct its full cost. Millions of Americans have surrendered their freedom to the tax system. For such people, every day—not just April 15th—is tax day. It is the ultimate intrusion of the income tax into people's lives.

The cost of all this professional assistance is estimated to be well over $1 billion a year. According to William Raby at the accounting firm of Touche, Ross & Company, the number of active tax professionals has increased 15 percent in the last two years to 46,000. Add to that the IRS personnel, the tax lawyers, secretaries, receptionists, bookkeepers and apprentices and you'll begin to understand that coping with the tax code is more than a cottage industry. It directly employs nearly 150,000 people.

There are more U.S. citizens in the tax business than in the Air Force and Marine Corp Reserves combined. It takes more people to prepare, strategize, mail, and examine the nation's 100 million tax returns each year than it does to teach English to all the students in all the colleges of America.

In many cases, the tax lawyers and accountants are among our most gifted intellectual talents. It's a shame that they couldn't devote more of their time to an activity which builds America instead of one that saps its internal strength. For make no mistake, that is what is happening with our tax system.

While these professionals generally do a good and honest job, the U.S. tax system has always depended on "self-assessment"—people figuring out what they owe and paying up voluntarily. The assumption of such a system was that the citizen, perhaps grumbling, recognized that he had to bear his fair share of government's costs just as he attended the schools, crossed the bridges, and rode the subways that government built.

If millions of Americans can't figure out their own tax liabilities, the foundation of that system is seriously undermined. Complexity goes hand-in-hand with the perception of unfairness.

As a result, we can no longer boast the kind of voluntary compliance that used to be the envy of the industrial world. Instead, we have an alarming amount of under-reporting as well as downright cheating and evasion. In 1981, the Internal Revenue Service estimated total unreported legal source income at about $250 billion.

From 1960 to 1980, most increases in government programs came in the form of either more generous entitlement payments to broad classes such as senior citizens or categorical grants to specific interest groups such as farmers or educators or mayors. People increasingly viewed government expenditures as going to someone other than them. There were fewer and fewer expenditures that everyone could see and connect with their level of taxes (like bridges or public buildings, for example). There were fewer expenditures that benefited everyone in the community in the same way. Instead, people were supposed to believe that even though they were helping to pay for special programs for one specific group or another, it all balanced out in the end.

But, of course, they didn't believe it. One reason people doubted that government would act in the general interest by spending equitably might have been because they saw the tax system becoming more and more unfair. The "specialization" of federal spending occurred at the same time as loopholes proliferated. The poor were taken care of through government appropriation; the rich were taken care of through tax manipulation and the middle class paid both bills. As inflation pushed middle-income people into higher tax brackets more citizens sought professional help in preparing their tax returns. By 1981, it seemed as if everyone had an accountant and said so, partly out of pride and partly out of fear.

The political effect of this phenomenon has been to divest a growing number of Americans from fulfilling their fundamental democratic duty of paying for the activities of government. When a citizen has little or no idea why he is taxed and sees no good results from the way his taxes are spent, he can become cynical about government. He readily tunes out his other democratic duty—voting. He becomes self-absorbed; convinced not only that his material comfort is all that matters, but that the blind pursuit of it cannot hurt the health of our democratic system. Government becomes just another obstacle to avoid or finesse on the path to success, even though the citizen knows that in a crisis he will have to turn to government to hold us all together.

A Yankelovich poll in 1981 asked: If you abide by the rules will you get ahead in America? An astonishing 81 percent of the American people said no! While that result reflects many trends, certainly one stems from the set of rules that affects 100 million taxpayers annually—the tax system. As long as the Code is so complicated that only experts can understand it, as long as almost as much money is excluded from tax collection as is collected (and for reasons that are never reexamined), and as long as the system produces widely disparate effects on similarly situated taxpayers, many Americans will remain convinced that you're a sucker if you play by the rules.

The feeling that each individual's special interest is inconsistent with the general interest—and more important than the general interest—demeans all of us.

There's got to be a better way.

CHAPTER 2

THE TAX LAW IS UNFAIR

(Why Your Neighbors Pay Less Tax Than You Do)

Meet auto mechanic Frank Pagani and art historian Kathy Barron. Both earned salaries of $20,999 last year, but Kathy had an additional income of $80,000 in interest on state industrial revenue bonds.

When Frank and Kathy completed their federal tax returns, they found that each owed the same amount to the government—even though Kathy's total income of $100,000 was five times bigger than Frank's.

The reason: they both had the same *taxable* income. Kathy's $80,000 in interest income was tax-free under a law that provides special treatment for bonds that states issue to promote industrial growth. It's a way of giving the appearance of low interest rates even when government economic policy has produced sky high real rates.

There's nothing illegal or even particularly unusual about the disparity in taxable income between Kathy and Frank. Kathy merely benefited from one of the more than 100 special provisions or "loopholes" in the Internal Revenue Code that allow people to reduce their tax liability. As a result, people, such as Frank and Kathy, with vastly *different* incomes often end up paying the *same* amount in taxes.

Conversely, people with the *same* incomes frequently find themselves paying *different* amounts of tax. Take the case of Jerry Stevenson and Jim Montaro. Each man had a $40,000 income last year; each has a wife and two young children. But when it came time to pay taxes, Jim paid about $1,620 less because his income included a $10,000 profit from the sale of corporate stock bought two years earlier. Under the law, 60 percent of Jim's gain in the stock venture—$6,000—was tax-free. So while Jerry paid taxes on his full income of $40,000, Jim paid taxes on only $34,000 of the $40,000 he made.

Some provisions of the Code are designed to benefit a specific group of people—such as Americans employed overseas. Walter Otlowski knew that, and it was a big factor in his decision to go to work for a cosmetics company in Europe. Currently the firm's top sales representative, Walter pulls down a $70,000 salary plus a $10,000 annual housing allowance for him and his family. But under our Code, Walter doesn't have to pay any U.S. taxes on his income—no matter how little he may pay in income taxes where he lives.

Some provisions are intended to counter the negative effect of other government policy decisions. The retirement credit for example is used primarily by retired federal workers. Its purpose was to compensate them for the fact that they paid more into their retirement system than the normal worker paid into Social Security and that their pension was taxable while Social Security payments were tax exempt. Now federal workers are under Social Security and some Social Security benefits are taxable, but the retirement credit still remains.

Some provisions such as nontaxable fringe benefits unwittingly place in the Code a potential pressure for higher rates. As tax rates get higher, workers often ask for a bigger share of their wages in the form of tax-free fringes. The most common benefits are health and life insurance, where the employer often pays half the cost of the employees' premiums. The employer's contribution is in fact income to the employees. It's as if they'd been given cash to purchase life and health insurance. The difference is that when the employer contributes directly to the insurance company, the value of the premiums isn't taxed. This can cause unfair results. If Tom Smith makes $15,000 a year, and his employer contributes $1,000 to his insurance on top of that, he pays $1,801 in taxes. If his neighbor Pete Jones earns $16,000, but gets no fringes, Pete will pay $2,001 in taxes. As fringes expand, the tax base is eroded further, leading to higher tax rates on a smaller base—and greater attempts to create even more elaborate nontaxable fringe benefits.

But there is a larger question here. Those who support the expansion of fringe benefits on the grounds that it replaces government expenditures with private payments don't fully realize that government is still involved. The Code, through its provisions, influences the relationship between employer and employee by what it defines as fringe benefits for tax purposes. Instead of allowing the worker (or his union) and management to structure their compensation package as they prefer, the government, by pushing them toward certain benefits, does it for them. Instead of having low tax rates for everyone with more after-tax dollars to buy anything from healthcare to helicopters, the present system allows the government to provide hidden benefits—as if the citizen is getting something for nothing. In the end though, we all will pay higher rates.

These are just a few of the tax preferences that have made their way into the Code over the years. In total there are 102 special provisions in the law that give benefits to some group. It is plausible to see each one, in isolation, serving some purpose larger than self-interest. But in total they leave the average taxpayer with higher rates and a lot more hassle. It is similar to the Civil War draft when a draftee had his choice of serving in the army or paying a fee. But even if he bought his way out, someone had to go to fight the war. With the income tax system, if *you* buy your way out by using loopholes, someone still has to pay the taxes and that leaves the rest of the taxpayers paying higher rates on *their* income.

All of us have to share in the adjustment necessary to create a tax system with lower rates for all Americans. Each of us will have to give up *something,* since most taxpayers benefit from one kind of tax preference or another. The wealthiest groups (those with income above $100,000) benefit enormously from the preferential treatment for capital gains. The highest rate on long-term capital gains is 20 percent, even though the people receiving the biggest share of that income would have to pay 50 percent on their wage, interest, or dividend income. This same group also receives most of the benefits from the tax-free status of interest on state and local government bonds.

Middle-income taxpayers (those in the $20,000–$50,000 range) benefit primarily from such deductions as those for mortgage interest, state and local taxes, consumer interest and medical expenses.

Low-income taxpayers are helped most by provisions such as the tax-exempt status of most Social Security benefits, the earned income and dependent care tax credits, and the additional exemption for the elderly.

So while people usually (and correctly) associate loopholes with the rich, in fact, every income group benefits to some extent from tax preferences.

On balance, however, deductions and exclusions are worth much more to high-bracket taxpayers than to those lower down the economic scale. A person's tax bracket, or "marginal" tax rate, is the amount of additional tax he or she will have to pay on each additional dollar of income. Today, these brackets range from 11 percent on the first $2,000 of taxable income to 50 percent on taxable income in excess of $81,800 for a single person and $162,400 for a married couple. Thus, when a high-income taxpayer in the 50-percent bracket pays his mortgage, or makes a charitable contribution, the government reduces his taxes by 50 cents for every dollar spent on interest or donations. He then has those "saved" tax dollars for other expenditures. But for a taxpayer in the 20-percent bracket, the government reduces his taxes by only 20 cents out of every dollar, with the taxpayer paying the remaining 80 cents. In other words, the rate of reduction in taxes is the taxpayer's marginal tax rate. This results in relatively generous treatment of the well-to-do, while providing much less for middle class taxpayers and nothing at all for the very poor—the income group with the greatest need of assistance.

Unfortunately, too, every provision that allows some taxpayers to exclude income from taxation turns into an opportunity for the minority of tax cheaters.

A friend who is a partner in one of the country's most prestigious tax law firms has a daughter who is about to graduate from the business school of a respected university. When asked what we should expect from her business school class, the future top executives of America, the daughter replied, "Frankly I've seen some things that disturb me. For instance almost everybody I know deducts the school's tuition as a business expense on their tax returns. I asked my dad about this and he said most tax experts consider it illegal. But the students do it anyway. Some of them admit that it's probably wrong, but are betting that they won't be caught. Others rationalize it and say 'it's really a deduction for keeping up job skills.' "

"But to claim that deduction you have to have a job already," one said. "If they're in business school, presumably they aren't holding down jobs too."

"Well," came the answer, "most of them had summer jobs. They say that going to business school improves the skills they need for those."

Her father said he'd be happy to recommend a good lawyer who specializes in defending people accused of criminal tax fraud—since that's what the students were doing.

The Internal Revenue Service announced recently that in 1981, there were $33 billion worth of overstated exemptions, expenses and deductions on tax returns. This translates into a tax revenue loss of about $13 billion.

One day, a woman came up to me incensed that her company was now withholding on the income she earned from going door to door selling cosmetics. When I asked her why she was upset, she said that now she'd have to declare her salary and that would push her husband and her into a higher bracket. She said she might as well quit working and glaring at me said, "When is the government going to leave me alone?"

Tax cheaters may always be with us. Try as it may,

the IRS can't detect every minor dodge; that would probably require giving tax examiners intrusive powers that the honest taxpayer would find excessive. But if all those unnecessary deductions weren't there, the chances for fraud would be less—and honest taxpayers such as Avon ladies who pay their taxes would bear a lighter burden, with lower and fewer rates of tax and much less bracket creep.

But tax cheating and nonreporting are not our only problem. The IRS has said that in 1981, 226 American families reported incomes of more than $200,000 and paid not one cent in taxes. The respected Brookings Institution has reported that the average effective tax rate for people earning more than $1 million a year is only 17.7 percent—less than many middle-class families pay.

The amazing thing is that those wealthy nontaxpayers probably aren't cheating. They're using provisions that have been written into the law for the express purpose of encouraging some people to avoid taxes while leaving the rest of us with high tax rates. They're called tax shelters. And they're worth a closer look.

CHAPTER 3

THE TAX LAW IS UNFAIR—CONTINUED

(True Tales of Amazing Tax Shelters)

Most of us have never seen one, will never own one, and wouldn't recognize one on the street. But tax shelters—investment schemes designed to allow some people to avoid paying their fair share in taxes—are a big business these days. In 1983 tax shelters soaked up more than $14 billion in investment capital. The Internal Revenue Service estimated that those shelters cost the federal government—and other taxpayers—more than $3.5 billion in lost revenue to say nothing of the lost jobs that could have been created if that $14 billion had been put to productive uses.

Tax shelters come in a dizzying variety of shapes and sizes. They can be railroad boxcars or sleek sailboats; beef cattle or thoroughbred race horses; coal mines or avocado groves; oil wells or art prints; billboards or bibles. An ad in one newspaper offered the following:

TAX SHELTERS THAT PAY

Do you like to sail? If you do and would like to spend your tax dollars for a sailboat, you should consider buying a new sailboat and placing it in charter with us. You can be eligible for a 10 percent Tax Interest Credit, interest deductions and a full year's depreciation to offset your income.

But they all have at least two characteristics in common: they fit into nooks and crannies of the tax law—and they're expensive. You have to be rich, or at least comfortable, to afford one.

That's the "Catch 22" for most taxpayers: the more money you have, the more tax shelters you can afford—and the more taxes you can avoid paying. At the extreme, one of the ten wealthiest people in the country, literally a billionaire, sheltered so much of his gigantic income between 1975 and 1977 that he paid a grand total of $9.65 in taxes. But there are plenty of less ambitious shelters; a recent article in *Fortune* magazine reported that a growing number of highly-paid executives are investing in show-horse farms and vacation homes, and deducting their costs as business expenses. The article was called "Having Fun Beating the Taxman."

So many tax shelters are being sold, in fact, that some of them are swindles—designed mainly to make money for their promoters, and only secondly to help the investors avoid taxes. One sad effect of our loss of confidence in the tax system is, it seems, that some people are willing to throw money away as long as they keep it out of the hands of the IRS.

THE FAIR TAX

The following true story involved an acquaintance of mine who is a tax lawyer.

Several years ago, on December 31st, a doctor raced into the lawyer's office and proclaimed, "My accountant just told me that I'm going to have to pay $50,000 in taxes. I don't have $50,000, but I do have $20,000. So here's a check made out in blank for the sum of $20,000. Please put me into something, anything so that I won't owe the IRS the $50,000 in taxes."

The "something, anything" that this "taxpayer" wants to be "put into" is called a tax shelter. He will take his chances in what is known as the "audit lottery," because the chances of being caught seem pretty low. The IRS doesn't audit every return, and even if one is targeted, the examining revenue agent must be expert enough to discover the questionable claim. If that happens, the taxpayer has an opportunity to negotiate with the IRS. If no compromise is reached, the taxpayer must go to trial; but a government attorney has to convince the court by making a persuasive argument in a complex case. Even if the taxpayer ultimately loses, he will have been earning interest on the taxes he should have paid when his tax return was due. So he still might come out ahead, even if he has to pay up. To show you how long it can take, I know of one government attorney who had two babies, not twins, during the course of litigating one tax appeal.

Is it any wonder, therefore, that the membership of the International Association of Financial Planners has increased 150 percent since 1979? Every day more and more Americans turn to tax planners for advice on tax shelters, and while ten years ago the IRS reviewed only 400 tax shelters, this year they are examining 327,000.

Here's how one typical tax shelter works. A taxpayer signs a contract to pay $150,000 for a number of art prints and the original lithographic plate from which they were made. But instead of paying $150,000 in cash, the taxpayer pays only $15,000 and signs an IOU to pay the other $135,000 later, from the proceeds of selling the prints. Why? Because under existing law, the taxpayer can deduct the entire $150,000 from his income! For a wealthy taxpayer in the 50 percent bracket, his $15,000 outlay could produce as much as $75,000 in tax savings. At that rate, the taxpayer doesn't really care whether the art prints are ever sold or not. So you can imagine the quality of the art.

Another example: The largest syndicated tax shelter in history allows the partners to purchase 45,000 old billboards for $485 million and depreciate them over the 15-year write-off period for real estate. When the billboards are sold, they will generate a long-term capital gain taxed at preferential rates. Each investor must put up $150,000, so this shelter is only available to the big hitters. However, each was promised net tax benefits over a six-year period worth $181,950; that is, the tax benefits exceeded the original investment. Is this what the President meant by supply-side economics? Obviously not. No economic growth results from simply reshuffling the ownership of 45,000 existing billboards.

Another example: Bennington College has been talking about selling its campus to its alumni and leasing it back. The Navy has been attempting to lease cargo ships and tankers from private owners for the rapid deployment force to be stationed in the Middle East. State and local governments have been selling their city halls, museums, convention centers, waste disposal facilities, sewer systems, and many other infrastructure investments to private investors and then leasing them back. Why? Because the 1981 tax act gave so big a benefit to those who invest in capital assets, many people are prepared to buy anything (even City Hall) to get the tax breaks, and many tax exempt organizations are selling their property with the tax benefits they can't use and then leasing it back. In each case, the costs to the Navy, to Bennington, or to the local government, are reduced because the private owners of the property will receive so much in tax benefits that they can afford to lease the property back at lower rents. However, the Treasury loses so much revenue as a result of these deals that the ultimate effect is simply to increase the budget deficit to put upward pressure on market interest rates and of course provide work for numerous lawyers, accountants, and investment bankers. By 1988 it is estimated that unless the law is changed, these deals will cost the Treasury $5 billion per year in lost revenue. It is outrageous to have a tax system that encourages universities, military units, and local governments to turn themselves into short-term tax shelters by literally selling themselves to the best-heeled bidder. If activities deserve public support, we ought to fund them up front.

Another example: Under the 1981 tax bill, business automobiles can be written off over three years—with a 6-percent investment credit in addition. Three years is probably an accurate lifetime for a taxicab; but it is probably much too short for an expensive car used by a doctor, lawyer, or other professional in the course of his business. Many such people buy expensive sedans and take big tax breaks and at the end of three years have a car that, far from being worn out, is worth more than when they started. So the next time you see a well-heeled-looking personage in a Rolls or a Mercedes, enjoy the view but contemplate that you might be helping him to pay for it—you and every other taxpayer in America.

Another example: Some types of real estate development depend so much on tax shelter investment that during debate in the Senate Finance Committee one day, Senator Bob Dole suggested simply exempting the industry from all tax. A giveaway? Not at all. According to the Treasury Department, rather than losing any money, exempting real estate from tax would *save* the government $15 billion a year. How? Simple. The $15 billion is the extra money that would be collected if we eliminated real estate tax preferences. No tax, no preference. In other words, taxpayers in general are subsidizing real estate investors to the tune of $15 billion every year.

Another example: A well-known Wall Street firm allegedly promotes an equipment purchase deal that yields handsome tax savings for those who sign up. While the deal is incredibly complex—the prospectus is about 85 pages long—its essence is simple. Assume that a manufacturer has a piece of equipment selling for $100,000. A user who simply bought that equipment would be able to deduct the $100,000 over five years as a depreciation allowance and claim an investment tax credit of $10,000 based on the $100,000 purchase price. This credit would be subtracted directly from taxes owed to the government. The $100,000 of depreciation would produce $50,000 in tax savings for a taxpayer in the 50 percent bracket.

As if that were not enough, under the Wall Street firm's tax shelter plan the manufacturer now says to the user, "Don't pay me the $100,000 up front. Instead, I'll lend you the $100,000 for 29 years at a stated interest rate of 9 percent."

"But," says the buyer, "the real interest rate is 11 percent."

"I know," says the seller. "We'll add that 2 percent spread, compounded annually for 29 years, to the selling price of the equipment. That pushes the price, believe it or not, to about $670,000 instead of $100,000. Your actual costs are the same—but you can figure your depreciation and investment tax credit on the $670,000 price. That means that your deductions will be worth almost seven times as much. The taxpayers as a whole will pay through the nose and you and I will split the proceeds."

Magic? No, just manipulation, and the rest of us taxpayers foot the bill for the inflated depreciation deductions and investment tax credits that were the sole point of this fancy financing.

As different as tax shelters may look, most of them share the same basic features. The main pillars of tax shelter schemes are claiming deductions far in excess of the actual cash investments; converting ordinary income into capital gains, which are taxed at lower rates; and deferring payment of taxes until several years after income is actually earned. Tax shelters also depend on the rules that allow taxpayers to combine all their income and losses on a single tax return and on the rules that govern a business arrangement called a "limited partnership."

There is nothing illegal about the above transactions. Congress approved all of them. Individuals seeking to avoid high tax rates and to get rich take advantage of these deals just as they would not hesitate to pick up a beautiful seashell on a walk along the seashore. But it is important to remember that it is the high general tax rates that force this kind of financial contortion. Wouldn't it be easier just to lower the tax rates and free up the minds that developed these tax avoidance schemes to think about ways to increase U.S. competitiveness, or just to get rich, without tax avoidance worries taking up to 25 percent of their time?

For all their other faults, tax shelters are habit-forming; once you start investing in one it's very difficult to stop. The reason is that many tax shelters don't really allow a taxpayer to avoid taxes altogether. Instead, they only enable him to put off the time of reckoning to a later year. So how does the taxpayer deal with these deferred tax bills? Simple, he invests in yet another tax shelter. So the problem never goes away, it just gets worse.

Some tax shelter activity does more harm than merely to distort investment decisions. It is one thing if a business buys a machine that isn't the best choice because of the tax law; but it is much more if investors and promoters ceaselessly swap worthless property to avoid taxes. When that starts to happen it can have dangerous repercussions for our economy, as was evident in the 1982 collapse of the Penn Square National Bank in Oklahoma. As the *Washington Post* reported:

> The high-bracket investors put up $37,500 and got $150,000 tax deductions. The high-risk wildcat oil companies put up relatively little and got millions of dollars to drill new wells. The high-flying bank got to pad its growing loan portfolio with loans that were to pay three points or more above the prime rate.
>
> The drilling partnerships seemed almost too good to be true. And many of them were.
>
> A series of such multi-million-dollar tax shel-

ter deals that went sour this spring helped pro-
pel the Oklahoma Penn Square National Bank
into insolvency.

In this case the investors were looking for tax shelters,
not real profits, so they didn't worry about the reliabil-
ity of the estimates of the reserves they were sup-
posedly investing in, and the bank didn't seek indepen-
dent appraisals.

The tax shelter investors got their deductions, but a
lot of others stand to suffer substantial losses. For
instance, 136 credit unions are expected to lose at least
$20 million of the $104 million in uninsured deposits
they had in the bank when it failed.

Some tax shelters go even far beyond what I've just
described. These "abusive" shelters frequently in-
volve activities that are downright illegal; their promoters are perpetrating criminal fraud. The most common of these abuses include backdating documents,
claiming deductions to which the taxpayer is not enti-
tled, claiming expenses for nonexistent assets, and
using foreign corporations or bank accounts to camou-
flage the nature of transactions and disguise the iden-
tity of the parties involved. According to U.S. Senate
investigators, in 1983 as much as $40 billion was
concealed through foreign bank accounts in the Carib-
bean alone. As IRS Commissioner Egger puts it,
"There's nothing legitimate about abusive shelters.
They are phony financial ploys to make promoters rich
and keep investors tax-free. The profits associated
with abusive shelters bring unscrupulous operators out
of the woodwork."

Just last year the IRS uncovered the biggest tax
fraud to date—$130 million in bogus deductions. The
promoters, New York securities dealers, set up two
limited partnerships to shelter investors' income by

generating losses from trading in government securities. The problem was that the transactions were largely phony and the documentation was all made up. The limited partners, many of whom were celebrities in the entertainment business, innocently relied on the fake documents in claiming losses on their own tax returns. For both 1979 and 1980 these deductions amounted to over $60 million.

As if all this wasn't enough, Congress, which should be working to eliminate most of the loopholes that allow these schemes, more often adds new ones. Most are the handiwork of the special interests, industries, groups, or individuals who found that adding a special section to the tax law was an easy way to save money. The trouble with those savings, of course, is that they are granted at the general expense—with little or no consideration of whether they are fair to the rest of us.

Internal Revenue Code Section 166(f) illustrates this point. This law allowed a bad debt deduction under certain highly specific circumstances. It is said that Section 166(f) was written for the benefit of a single businessman. The provision was repealed in 1976, presumably after having taken care of its beneficiary's needs.

Other examples of such special relief are a provision benefiting a single company and its employees with regard to stock options, a provision that saved about $2 million in taxes for a retired executive of a well-known corporation, and another that resulted in $4 million in tax savings for the estate of a wealthy widow.

There is nothing wrong with people getting rich; in fact, it's good for the country. But there is no reason why wealthy people should be enriched further with gimmicks whose general costs are hidden at the expense of high rates for the rest of us. Once that position is put frequently and widely enough, the people can decide between tax shelters or low tax rates.

The legislator sponsoring loophole legislation doesn't usually aim at satisfying a wealthy constituent or a greedy special interest. He may have the highest motives and believe ardently in the merits of his cause. As I've said, a provision in isolation can have a noble if vague purpose such as promoting energy independence or adequate housing or jobs. I myself have pushed amendments to tax bills that others have rightly described as special interest provisions. In 1981, I pushed the R&D tax credit that benefited universities and companies with big research budgets. In the 1982 tax bill, I worked to ensure that urban mass transit would receive highly preferential treatment. I did so because I believed that the Code was the only vehicle available for ensuring adequate funding to projects that are vital to the economic well-being of New Jersey. How, then, could I expect others to do any less for their state or district?

The collective discipline to resist offering special interest provisions can only develop when we have something more appealing to offer to the politician and to the citizen than yet another favor through the tax law. But if we can't develop that discipline among the wealthy beneficiaries of tax favors, how can we expect, as a democracy, discipline among the poor and middle class who look for more and more government assistance. Our history has shown that discipline across the economic spectrum is rarely easy. But now, there has never been more at stake.

CHAPTER 4

INEFFICIENCY

America will never produce jobs for all its citizens unless we compete effectively in a growing world economy. At the same time we protect the stability of that world economy, we must prepare ourselves for its competition.

To protect economic stability will take leadership precisely at a time when our relative strength is waning. America is still the largest and strongest economy but there are others growing rapidly and challenging our predominance. Thirty years ago, if our national government followed wrong-headed economic policies, other countries weren't able to take advantage of them for their own purposes. Today when our interest rates go up, it seems, even though everyone is damaged in the long run, many countries can play off our mistakes to enhance their short-term position at our expense. The result is a smaller margin for error in our economic policy.

To prepare ourselves for international competition requires discipline. In the past when nations did not have the discipline to succeed within a set of accepted trade rules, they broke the rules. Those violations led to further erosion of economic stability, and in some extreme cases, as worldwide economic conditions deteriorated, they led to war. To avoid that path America must discipline itself to compete effectively. We must insist on the most efficient possible allocation of our resources. We cannot expect to continue squandering our national wealth and remain competitive. Investments must be made in ways that increase our overall competitive position.

The present income tax system rewards inefficiency. It encourages people to lose money for tax reasons. It encourages investments that do not contribute to U.S. competitiveness. It encourages special interests to ask for more and more incentives—either to do what they should be doing anyway, or to continue what they have been doing only because of the overly generous incentives they already have. We need a breed of entrepreneurs willing to treat risk as an opportunity and not a threat. The market, not the tax-writing committees of Congress, is the most efficient allocater of resources. That's why our present tax system must go. It prevents us from reaching our economic potential as a nation.

High Tax Rates

So how does the tax law keep our economy from being what it could be?

First of all, it imposes excessively high tax rates on every productive activity, including work, saving, and investment. A family making $40,000 can easily be in the 30-percent tax rate bracket—so an extra dollar of income brings home only 70 cents after federal income taxes. The highest rate is 50 percent, so only half of every extra dollar of income makes it home. If that extra pay comes hard—through overtime, a second job, a promotion with added responsibility—the payoff might not seem worth the effort. So the tax system discourages us as individuals from working as hard as we could.

The same can be true of business. A corporation that makes a product breakthrough can be faced with high tax rates—the highest rate on corporations is 46 percent. The incentive to take a chance is certainly dulled if almost half of the prize goes to someone else. And the firm that has been successful can't plow back into research and internal risk-taking as much of the fruits of that success when tax rates are high.

So both businesses and workers are hurt when tax rates are as high as ours. There is no need for the high tax rates we have.

The Tax Law and Business Investment

Haven't we recognized the problems of high tax rates? Yes, we have, but we have responded to it in a very counterproductive way.

We haven't addressed the problem of high tax rates as a society, with the interests of the whole economy in mind. Rather, we have taken it on one interest at a time, year in and year out.

Every imaginable group of individuals and businesses has felt the pain of high tax rates on its own particular activity and industry. And many of these groups came to Washington and asked their elected representatives for relief—*selective* relief, an exclusion, deduction, or credit to suit their individual needs. The most powerful and influential got what they wanted.

The resulting array of preferential tax provisions— loopholes—has many negative effects. They cost the Treasury revenue, and thereby *keep* tax rates high in order to raise the necessary funds for government. They unfairly benefit those Americans who can take advantage of them compared to those who can't. They complicate the tax law.

But here, I'd like to talk about one key effect: how the loopholes influence business investment, and what that does to the efficiency of the economy.

Think of an investor—someone who wants to put some money to work for him. He doesn't want to play games with the tax law; he just wants to do business in the good old free-enterprise tradition.

This investor wants the highest rate of return on his investment. Whether he has $1,000 or $100,000, or $1,000,000, he asks the same question: "Which investment will make the most money?" In making the decision to invest in a company's stock, for example, he looks to see whether the firm is doing a good job, whether there is a demand for its product, whether its management structure can sustain its performance, and whether the workers are quality oriented. All of these judgments determine whether he makes the investment. This kind of calculation also maximizes our national comparative advantage, because under it capital flows to the companies that have the highest level of potential earnings over a long period against worldwide competition.

Unfortunately, the tax system intervenes between the investor and the ultimate investment. It skews the rates of return so that investors frequently don't put their money into the company or investment with the greatest potential earnings in the marketplace.

How? When the investor looks at the available investment alternatives, the tax law biases the bottom line. No matter how good an oil well looks in the marketplace, the tax law makes it look better—with special deductions for intangible drilling costs and percentage depletion. Whatever profit timber production will generate, the tax law makes it larger—with special capital gains exclusions on some income. Whatever the rate of return on a bank, the tax law makes it higher—with extra deductions for bad debt losses, even if there are no bad debts. And there are many more.

So the investor puts his money not where the marketplace tells him, but where the tax law tells him. But in a competitive world economy, it is the marketplace that measures success. A tax deduction won't help you if a firm from Japan or West Germany comes in with a product that consumers here or abroad like better, and you have no income from which to subtract your deduction.

The tax system interferes with business decisions in every industry. The 1981 tax bill, for example, removes any incentive for businesses to invest only in machines that enhance their competitiveness. By allowing businesses to deduct the costs of virtually all their machines over the same length of time—regardless of how long the machines will in fact last, the tax law encourages firms to buy some machines that do not yield the maximum efficiency in the production of goods or services but rather the maximum tax savings on April 15. With the reward in the marketplace gone for modernizing in an intelligent way, firms become less competitive than they could otherwise be.

The same kind of problem arises with respect to buildings. Under the 1981 tax cuts, the costs of buildings can be deducted over 15 years, even though the typical building lasts many times as long; you probably live in a building that is more than 15 years old. This short deduction period is a tremendous tax advantage; it probably means that we will have many more office and apartment buildings. We certainly want good offices and apartments, but there is a definite tradeoff against other priorities—do we want to be the best-housed and -officed people in the world, but with the 17th best jobs and factories? If our jobs and factories are 17th best, our housing and offices won't stay the best for long.

Some people say that we can only make our economy more efficient through some kind of an *industrial policy*—direct government involvement in investment banking, long-term planning, job training and retraining, and labor-management relations. Industrial policy has become a controversial issue. But *advocates and opponents* agree that we already have a kind of industrial policy—in the Internal Revenue Code. The array of special industry tax provisions, including the 1981 business tax cuts, are haphazard government influences on business decisions. They helped get us into the mess we are in today that has given us a two-tiered recovery and a gigantic time-bomb of a deficit ticking into our children's future. If we want a better industrial policy—or if we don't want an industrial policy at all—we must start by eliminating these biased provisions in our current tax code, and leaving a tax law that doesn't distort business decisions. Then we can add a targeted national industrial policy, or not, as we see fit. So whether you're for the market to allocate our resources or whether you're for an active government intervention to shape our economic structure, both approaches require clearing out the underbrush of tax provisions that respectively impede the functioning of the market or the ability of government to target investment incentives more effectively.

I'll talk about these business tax questions again later, in another context. But for now, the lesson is very clear: the tax law makes us less competitive in the world economy.

What Is at Stake

There is more at stake in this discussion than fine points of economic theory. Without economic growth and full employment we cannot have rising standards of living for working people and prosperity for investors. Without economic growth and full employment we cannot fulfill our promises to the poor, the elderly, and the disabled, or achieve the highest standards of living for our working people and investors. When the economy stagnates. one group is pitted against another in a battle of attrition. As times get worse, the common good of the community or nation is sacrificed to the special, narrow, selfish interest of the group or individual. If there isn't enough to go around, each grabs for his own. Each interest group thinks that it can get more at the expense of others through political clout. The inevitable result is either paralysis or polarization. Our democracy does not allocate sacrifice very well. Only when the economic pie is expanding can we assure full employment, adequate government services, and the prospect of a better tomorrow.

The foundation for future growth is the saving and investing we do today. A family that invests in a child's education will have a child better able to deal with the uncertainties of tomorrow, but a nation that fails to invest in new plants and technology will not have the means to compete tomorrow. The challenge is to match the investor's desire for a profit with the investment that will maximize national economic growth.

Right now our business sector is losing the lead in many segments of our own market—the largest market in the world. The reason is that other economies have learned to produce some products with higher quality and at a lower cost, even bearing the expense of shipping their goods here. Now there is no reason why we should produce *everything* we consume; as a world leader, we should be doing the jobs that require the most skill. But we must hold our own here at home, and, in an increasingly competitive environment, do our share of the business around the world.

To succeed in this competitive world economy we must be on the cutting edge of technological change, and we must be able to make the human adjustment at home to shift our labor and capital to the industries where we have the greatest competitive advantage.

With a limited pool of investment capital, we cannot afford to waste it on projects that generate profit only because of loopholes in the tax law—loopholes enacted because of the political clout of special interest groups, or because the Congress thought that it knew more than the marketplace.

Our system of tax subsidies leads to inefficiency in the allocation of capital; but our prospects for economic growth and full employment depend on our ability to compete in international markets. In a time of slow growth, such a system only intensifies the danger that special groups will take care of themselves at the expense of the general welfare. For both our prosperity and well-being as a society, we need a tax system that puts the general interest first.

CHAPTER 5

THE PROCESS

(So How Come the Tax Law Is Such a Mess?)

It has been said, accurately I might add, that "Laws, like sausages, cease to inspire respect in proportion as we know how they are made."

The process usually begins with the President announcing that he will shortly send a major tax bill to Congress.

Although that original package of proposals tends to be fairly spartan, it doesn't stay that way for long. Members of Congress and countless special interest lobbyists sieze the opportunity to use any tax bill for their own purposes. (The tax bill of 1980 began with a tariff bill exempting from import duty the bell clapper of the Foundry United Methodist Church of Washington, D.C.) "The train's at the station," they say, "and everybody better hop on board." Some people want to add totally unrelated provisions. Others either want to get a specific group included in the list of those receiving favorable treatment or stricken from the list of those losing existing benefits. Some merely want to delay the date on which a provision takes effect so they can complete a deal that would be prohibited by the new law. In sum, depending on whether it's a tax cut or a tax increase, people want in or out, more or less, sooner or later, or not at all. But they're all singing the little ditty made famous by Democratic Senator Russell Long of Louisiana when he was Chairman of the Senate Finance Committee: "Don't tax you, don't tax me, tax that fellow behind the tree."

Before the Senate Finance Committee begins writing the President's proposals into law, it holds hearings so that people opposing or supporting particular provisions can comment and suggest modifications. While any member of the public can request to testify, the special interests are invariably better represented than the average taxpayer. After the Senators who want to testify and after the Administration's witnesses who have been asked to testify, the well-paid representatives of the Washington trade associations give their views of the issue and finally, in most cases, after TV cameras have left and few Senators remain, the spokespersons for the general interest will testify.

At the same time, most Committee members and their staffs privately receive "petitioners." They commonly get 50 to 100 phone calls a day from people conveying views or requesting appointments to discuss certain provisions. The mail increases too, sometimes running as high as 8,000 letters a week—on tax proposals alone. Needless to say, all lobbyists assert unequivocally that the interests they represent are like motherhood and apple pie—good for, if not critical to, the well-being of the economy. They tell a logical story—not always the truth, but a logical story.

The lobbyists also claim that it won't cost much to approve whatever proposal they are pushing. Their calculation is frequently based on the so-called "feedback effect." For example, take a 10-percent tax credit for purchasing an American-made automobile. While the revenue loss caused by this credit would be billions of dollars over several years, the proponents of this type of legislation invariably argue that the credit will pay for itself. It will accomplish this amazing feat by boosting demand for American autos. This in turn will create thousands of new jobs and the people working in those jobs will be paying taxes rather than drawing unemployment and costing the taxpayers money. In three years, the proponents insist, a new U.S. automobile tax credit will have more than paid for itself.

It sounds plausible until someone suggests, "If a 10-percent credit will pay for itself in three years, why not make it 20 percent and pay for it in 18 months?" Indeed, if the analysis is correct, why not give a 50-percent credit and use the surplus revenue to help reduce the deficit? Somewhere in this chain of reasoning the logic is flawed.

The problem is, each argument is bolstered by its own analysis which always puts its particular special interest in the best possible light. And notwithstanding the expert professionals Congress relies on for its revenue estimates, politicians often tend to believe what they want to hear. With everyone wrapping himself in the flag and claiming his special interest can be taken care of at the most modest cost, is it any wonder our tax bills turn into Christmas trees?

A Tax Law Is Made

Let's take the Economic Recovery Tax Act, or ERTA, that President Reagan proposed in 1981. ERTA started out with only two essential components—three years of 10-percent across-the-board rate cuts for individuals and an extremely generous revision of the depreciation allowance for businesses. ERTA was, in the jargon of the Hill, a "clean" bill. It didn't stay that way for long. By the time the President signed it, ERTA had become, in the words of the *Baltimore Sun*, "a measure laced with special tax breaks for heirs, oilmen, industrial researchers, savings and loan associations, truckers, working wives and Americans employed overseas." A *New York Times* editorial said: "Greed and politics are running wild on Capitol Hill, and the Nation's great economic difficulties, which were supposed to be the object of budget and tax reductions, are recklessly ignored."

Instead of a tax cut that would have cost $340 billion over five years as President Reagan intended initially, the one we ended up with had a price tag of $754 billion—the biggest tax cut in history. The resultant deficits, high interest rates, and deep recession, while predictable, were not faced up to during the rush to give the President and the special interests everything they wanted.

From the beginning, ERTA promised to be the granddaddy of tax giveaways. The lobbyists' attempts to fatten the bill got an unusual boost from the politics of the situation. The Democrats in the Senate, newly out of power and uncertain how to respond to the Reagan Administration's tax cut initiative, decided to come up with an alternative. It would not be a challenge to the idea that we needed a tax cut, nor would it be a bold, new approach to the income tax system. Instead, it would accept unwittingly much of the President's conceptual framework about tax cuts producing more, not less revenue, and it would simply attempt to draw a contrast between how Democrats and Republicans cut taxes. Its key provision in the Senate was a personal income tax reduction that, unlike the across-the-board Republican version, would have given a bigger share of the tax relief to low- and middle-income Americans.

In the House, to build a coalition for their alternative, Democrats added a slew of high-priced "sweeteners." Industries that were not profitable enough to pay taxes—and so couldn't take advantage of the bill's rich investment tax credit and depreciation deductions—got a provision allowing them to sell their unused tax benefits to profitable companies looking for ways to shelter their income from tax. This ended up as the infamous "leasing" law, widely lambasted as corporate welfare and subsequently modified in the 1982 tax increase bill.

Both Republicans and Democrats tried to help the ailing savings and loan industry, which stated that it preferred the less generous Republican proposal because they offered their help first. Beyond showing honor among lobbyists (or realism, given the Republican White House) it demonstrated how arbitrary are decisions in the process even by those deriving the benefits. Oilmen, commodity traders, truckers, horse breeders, farmers, small businessmen, universities, and many other groups also pressed their case with impassioned intensity.

The Administration initially resisted this "something for everyone" approach, but then the pressure started to build. The promise of a second bill to take care of these special interest items failed to assuage the appetites of those who knew that it was only a ploy to keep them at bay. Sensing the potential for a bidding war between the Democrats and Republicans on the two tax-writing committees, the lobbyists turned up the heat. As Senator Dole himself remarked, in a candid acknowledgment of political reality, "When we want a cab, most of us take the first one in line."

Then the President, for unknown reasons, decided to abandon his "clean bill" principles. He vigorously joined the crowd supporting special interest provisions. This put the Democrats in a bind. With the President now supporting the special interest tax breaks, the Democrats had to raise the stakes. The general interest was the clear loser. Propelled by the President's endorsement, lobbying efforts went into high gear. In the House it was like a frantic auction. As the publication *Tax Notes* put it, "carefully primed grass-roots interests began to bombard congressional offices with phone calls supporting the President's tax cuts. . . . And when it became apparent that most of Georgia's Democratic delegation would vote with the Administration in return for promises of protection for Georgia's peanut crop, lobbyists say that the Administration gained the momentum it needed to rack up its third major legislative victory."

During the Senate mark-up of the bill, the hearing room was the scene of frenzied activity. People were rushing around trying to get the attention of a Senator or his staff; secretaries were constantly bringing in phone messages from lobbyists petitioning for last-minute favors; Treasury officials huddled in clumps doing revenue estimates on scraps of paper; amendments were drafted, circulated, and redrafted. Those who had been lucky enough to get in the hearing room became claustrophobic and struggled to get out, but every vacated place was immediately filled by someone from the long line outside the door. Deals were offered, and compromises were struck. The final vote was 19 to 1 for the bill.* A few days later a similar scene was staged on the floor of the Senate.

The Washington Post summed it all up this way: "We had hoped that the Administration might exert a calming influence on the great Christmas tree trimming party that the House and Senate have made of the tax bill . . . but instead, the Administration joined in the merriment . . . by adding its name to the card on some of Congress's favorite giveaways—doodads like the 'all-savers certificate,' the near wipe-out of the estate tax and continued absolution from taxation for the commodity speculators. It then added literally uncounted billions of dollars to the already munificent gifts planned for the oil industry."

President Reagan argued that all of these loopholes, plus his tax rate cuts, would so stimulate the economy that they would *increase government revenues*. These additional revenues would pay for a big defense buildup and balance the budget besides. But now, three years later, revenues are more than $100 billion below President Reagan's projections in his first budget submission to the Congress. We have added over $600 billion to the national debt since 1981 and we are facing huge budget deficits that won't quit, as far as the eye can see.

There may be a connection. Both spending *and* tax cuts create deficits just as sure as the two blades of the scissors cut the paper.

A Tax Law Isn't Reviewed

The chances that an ill-begotten tax law would ever

---

*I was the one.

be changed are not very great, in the normal course of legislative affairs.

The legislative process doesn't work like decision-making in the private sector. Businesses look at an investment to judge how profitable it will be over time in light of the company's financial condition and market environment. They invest the firm's capital in those projects which earn the highest rate of return, expand market share, or pave the way for new products and processes. Time and the market tell them whether they were right or wrong.

If the investment does not perform as well as expected, the manager who launched it is called on to explain why his original estimates were too optimistic; why the marketing plan didn't result in more sales; why the new equipment is underutilized; why there have been no breakthroughs from the increased research and development expenditures; why the costly worker retraining has not increased productivity.

In well-managed firms, project managers are rewarded or punished, based on how successfully their projects perform. If they meet the performance criteria, there is a bonus. If they exceed those criteria, there may be a super bonus. But if they fall short, not only is there no bonus, there is also the threat of being demoted or fired.

In small firms, there is even less margin for error. If a drycleaner borrows money to buy a new machine and it doesn't cut costs, he doesn't have the other lines of business that a big, diversified firm can fall back on. He may end up in bankruptcy. The marketplace disciplines small businessmen in a very straightforward way.

In contrast, once a tax incentive is enacted, there are no established oversight mechanisms to evaluate it. Occasionally provisions expire automatically at the end of a given period unless they are reenacted, but this is the exception, not the rule.

When Congress' tax-writing committees decide on a project, it can skew investment calculations for a whole industry, maybe the whole economy. The tax incentives can be created for one purpose, outlive that need and then spawn additional tax breaks. If the committees make mistakes—and they do—the errors tend to live much longer than those in the private sector.

For example, take the oil and gas percentage depletion allowance. This extremely generous tax break started out in 1918 largely as a World War I emergency measure to encourage the drilling of new oil wells to fuel the war effort. But, by the time the Act finally passed Congress in 1919, the war was over. This, of course, did not deter Congress from responding to the entreaties of the oil lobby. Over the years, the oil depletion allowance has encouraged other special interests to seek comparable relief, which the legislators from the oil states have supported for fear that otherwise, the non-oil states will oppose oil depletion. As a result, we now have a depletion allowance for over 100 different minerals, including such "minerals" as "oyster and clam shells," talc, asbestos, gravel, pumice, sand, scoria, wollastonite, kyanite, olivine, celestinite, corundum, tantalum, nepheline, syenite, and many more. There is even a special rule applying to clay used to make flowerpots.

If Congress, back in World War I, had decided to try to assist the oil industry through a direct spending program, the program would have been terminated shortly after the war and we would not be saddled with all these depletion allowances. The revenue loss from the depletion allowances requires higher tax rates for taxpayers outside the oil and mineral industries.

Take another example: the various tax breaks for alternative energy sources and technologies. These were added in 1977 because the Administration apparently believed that the world was on the verge of exhausting its oil and gas supplies. This policy was flawed on several counts. In the first place, oil and gas resources were not about to be depleted. Gas, in particular, has proven to be much more abundant than people believed. In the second place, if these resources were on the point of exhaustion, the price of oil and gas would have risen sharply and stayed high. These higher prices in and of themselves would have attracted substantial investment capital into producing alternatives to the scarce fuels. And in this case, tax subsidies would have been unnecessary. It would have been a waste of the general taxpayers' dollars to reward investors for doing what they would have done anyway—at a profit.

As it turned out, the "energy crisis" was due to oil supply disruptions, not resource depletion. The price surge caused by these supply disruptions induced a boom in oil and gas exploration and development. Supplies became more abundant. Prices stabilized, then declined. And the market for high-priced alternatives to oil and gas slumped.

With demand for alternative energy flagging, investors in these technologies became still more insistent on the need for "incentives." Since the market had lost its enthusiasm for their products, it was up to Congress to stimulate the supply by expanding the tax breaks. That way, taxpayers in general would subsidize select consumers and the investors in alternative energy would be insulated from market forces. In other words, they would be assured a high after-tax rate of return regardless of the investment's value in the marketplace.

Now I'm not against all government subsidies. I believe the public sector should pay for R&D on a wide range of activities such as energy, space, medicine, and agriculture. The reason is that the payoff from R&D is generally quite remote and highly speculative. Since the private sector's bottom line is profits, there's only so much they can and should do in R&D where relatively few projects ultimately pay off. Making up the difference is an appropriate role for government.

But there's an important difference between financing basic research that otherwise wouldn't get done and subsidizing the demonstration or commercial application of products and processes whose risks and paybacks are relatively well-known. In most cases, energy tax credits do the latter. They don't provide much help to the energy source that's still at the threshold of theoretical or engineering knowledge, such as nuclear fusion. Instead, they artificially boost the returns to processes or products on the verge of commercial viability or already on the market.

Even if such subsidies could be justified when the economy was flush, they are surely highly questionable when our economy is in disarray and our tax dollars have to finance more pressing public needs.

People act in reliance on a tax incentive, and the total of tax incentives becomes the base from which they plan. For example, incentives for oil production affect the expected returns not just of oil producers, but of all the firms that use oil or produce products that use oil. These people are a potent political force whose interests can't easily be brushed aside in the name of efficiency. But given the scarcity of investment capital, this failure to evaluate the effectiveness of tax incentives means that many more worthwhile public investment opportunities will be neglected.

The problem is made worse by the way we go about developing the federal budget. At present, the budget process does not include any limit on tax expenditures, such as oil depletion, even though 1981 tax expenditures for energy exceeded direct outlays, and tax expenditures for housing exceeded direct federal spending on housing four to one. Until we evaluate tax incentives alongside direct spending programs, we will be hampered in making well-informed choices about how best to spend the public's money.

The least we can do is stop hiding from the American people what and whom their government subsidizes. Every year there are big budget debates on what the federal government will authorize and appropriate. All the press stories focus on these numbers in the budget. "There is a $200 billion budget deficit." "Deficit spending is up." "Spending for education is down." What the press neglects to tell you is what is spent through the tax code. A first step toward getting control of tax preferences would be a unified budget, which clearly lays out what government spends not only through the authorization and appropriations process, but also through the tax code and off budget. Once all those numbers are laid out, the people could better determine what activities government should increase and reduce.

The Bottom Line

So our tax laws are made under incredible pressures, most of which run counter to the general interest, and old tax laws seldom, if ever, die. With the tax legislative process working so poorly, it's not surprising that the tax system is as unfair, complex, and inefficient as the preceding chapters have indicated.

The next chapter takes a longer-term view of how the tax law has evolved, and shows step by step how we got to where we are.

CHAPTER 6

HOW WE GOT THERE

(A Brief History of the Income Tax)

Ironically, the income tax most Americans now castigate as unfair was originally enacted to bring a measure of fairness to the tax system. The federal income tax has been run down by years of uncorrected bad habits, lots of well-intentioned tinkering, and some unexpected clashes with other economic policies.

Roots: The Civil War

Until the first U.S. income tax was enacted in 1861 to help finance the Civil War, federal revenues were collected through excise taxes and customs duties on imported goods such as coffee, tea, iron, cotton, woolen goods, and general manufactured products. For the average American family, living on what was, by today's standards, a meager income, it was a terribly unfair tax system. The wealthiest people paid little tax in relation to their incomes. The average citizen paid a very high share of the total taxes collected. He had to spend most of his earnings on the goods that were taxed while the very wealthy spent much less of what they took in on these necessities, saving the rest. In addition, wealthy manufacturers lobbied for high tariffs to hold domestic prices up and to make competing imports more expensive. One of the early tariff laws of the 19th century, passed in 1828, was so oppressive that it came to be known as the "Tariff of Abominations."

So in 1861, when it became clear that the Union would have to raise large sums to pay for its war efforts, there was a wave of interest in an income tax that would put at least part of the extra tax burden on those with the greatest ability to pay. Under the pressure of a growing war debt, the Congress finally settled on a tax of 3 percent on incomes below $10,000 and 5 percent of incomes above that level with a $600 exemption. President Lincoln signed the bill into law on July 1, 1862. The tax rates were increased, to range from 5 to 10 percent in 1864, when the finances of the Union were weakest.

The Civil War income tax was quite successful. Even though not taxing the first $600 of income meant that only the wealthiest persons paid any tax at all, the income tax raised over 18 percent of total federal revenues by the end of the War. Many people wanted the income tax continued after the war to balance the heavy burden of excises and tariffs on foreign imports. But despite its success, or perhaps because of it, the income tax came under heavy attack. Bills to continue the tax were invariably restricted to only a few years at a time. Opponents decried the tax, as in the words of Representative Dennis McCarthy of New York, "unequal, perjury-provoking and crime-encouraging, because it is at war with the right of a person to keep private and regulate his business affairs and financial matters," or as having "a socialistic tendency . . . a tax imposed expressly on the rich, and capable of indefinite expansion and class graduation." Senator John Sherman of Ohio answered these objections on the Senate floor in 1871:

When you come to examine the income tax you will find that it applies, it is true, to only about sixty thousand people; but they do not pay their proper share of other taxes. Why? Can a rich man with an overflowing revenue consume more sugar or coffee or tea, or drink more beer or whiskey, or chew more tobacco, than a poor man? You tax tobacco at the same rate per pound, whether it is tobacco for the wealthiest or the poorest. . . . But when in a system of taxation you are compelled to reach out to many objects, you must endeavor to equalize your general result. . . . Therefore, when it is complained that the tax on an article consumed is unjust upon the poor, because the poor have to consume a greater proportion of their income in its purchase than the rich, we answer that to countervail that we have levied a reasonable income tax upon such incomes as are above the wants and necessities of life. That is the only answer and it is a complete answer; because, if you leave your system of taxation to rest solely upon consumption, without any tax upon property or income, you do make an unequal and unjust system.

Sherman's words, and those of others, failed to earn a further renewal of the income tax. The tax law expired in 1872.

The Campaign to Reenact the Income Tax

The truth of Sherman's argument, however, became more evident over the following years. Strong political movements, including farmers associations, organized labor, and a revitalized Democratic party, arose in opposition to the excesses of tariff protection and the unfairness of its burden on the average citizen. Sixty-eight different income tax bills, introduced in Congress between 1873 and 1893, faltered in part due to pressure from the beneficiaries of the tariff system. But years of economic boom and bust, plus rising tariffs, brought the issue to a head. An economic panic and depression in 1893 resulted in action on the protective tariffs. Reducing the tariffs required raising other taxes to make up the lost revenue. A tax of 2 percent on incomes over $4,000 was offered as an amendment to a tariff bill in January of 1894, touching off one of the memorable debates in the history of the House of Representatives. Opponents argued that because the majority of the voters would not pay income taxes (due to the exemption of the first $4,000 of income), they would thereby lose their right to control the government. To that William Jennings Bryan replied, "If taxation is a badge of free men, let me assure my friend that the poor people of this country are covered all over with the insignia of free men. Notwithstanding the exemption imposed by this bill, the people whose incomes are less than $4,000 will still contribute far more than their just share to the support of the Government."

A group of prominent citizens had actually threatened to leave the country if an income tax were levied. To that, Bryan said:

> Of all the mean men I have ever known, I have never known one so mean that I would be willing to say of him that his patriotism was less than 2 percent deep. . . . If "some of our best people" prefer to leave the country rather than pay a tax of 2 percent, God pity the worst . . . we can better afford to lose them and their fortunes than risk the contaminating influence of their presence.

After intricate political maneuvering, the income tax was enacted in 1894 as part of a compromise tariff law. But before a dollar could be collected, the Supreme Court ruled that the income tax violated Article I of the Constitution, which says that all direct taxes must be levied among the states in proportion to their population. The Court's final vote on the issue was five to four.

Amending the Constitution

After 20 years of effort to reenact the income tax, the process was not only set back to the beginning; the task was to amend the Constitution. Many members of Congress did not accept that fact; they believed that the Supreme Court's decision was wrong, and that if confronted with a new income tax law from an insistent Congress the Court would be forced to reverse itself. But the weight of the Court's decision kept the supporters of the income tax from approaching a congressional majority until 1909. Again, the impetus for the income tax movement was bad economic news— this time, the Panic of 1907. As then-Congressman Cordell Hull described the situation:

> Many years of a protective tariff, with the train of evils that always follow in its wake, gradually created so many abnormal, unnatural, and artificial conditions in the country's financial, commercial, and industrial affairs that the panic of 1907–8 came as a natural outgrowth thereof. During this period of trial and suffering . . . the wail of distress and the constant cry for cheaper food, cheaper clothing, and cheaper shelter was loud and growing louder.

So again, there was pressure to reduce the protectionist tariffs, and again revenue would be needed to pick up the resulting slack. To the surprise of many, an income tax bill began to gather considerable momentum.

The income tax opponents found that their only defense was to offer to support a constitutional amendment. From the opponents' point of view, this seemed like good politics: if an income tax law were to pass, it might have gained approval from the Supreme Court, but a constitutional amendment, even after passage by Congress, required ratification by three-fourths of the states—a massive task.

Yet nearly everyone in the end supported the constitutional amendment. The reason was that both the ardent income tax supporters like Hull, and their opponents who thought state ratification unlikely, were joined by a third group that favored the tax but hesitated to make a frontal assault on the Supreme Court. Among the most persuasive who advocated the straight and narrow amendment path was President William Howard Taft himself. His campaign statements on the desirability and constitutionality of an income tax had always confounded his conservative friends, although most of them probably concluded that the candidate was merely trying to hold the political center. Now the President came out for an income tax in earnest, but he voiced concerns for public confidence in the Court if a crisis ensued, and so made his proposal in the form of an amendment to the Constitution. This proposal was coupled with a 2 percent tax on net income of corporations that won over many of the income tax advocates, such as Hull, who were also unsure of the Court's eventual ruling on a pure income tax bill.

After congressional passage, the real surprise was that ratification of the amendment advanced rapidly. By February of 1913 forty-two states—six more than needed—had ratified the amendment. The constitutional hurdle had been overcome, but there still remained the considerable task of legislating the income tax itself.

The Income Tax Is Reenacted

Under the leadership of the new Democratic President, Woodrow Wilson, the Congress went to work on a comprehensive tariff reform and income tax bill in 1913. Wilson's effort was crucial; he twice intervened firmly when he felt that the tariff reform was getting off the track, and in the end the tariff reform was genuine. Cordell Hull was given the task of drafting an income tax law to replace most of the $100 million lost in the tariff reduction. Hull began:

Mr. Chairman, for many years those who believe in justice in taxation have been striving to secure the adoption of a national income tax. . . .

. . . The very fact that this is a just tax means that it will meet with opposition; the beneficiaries of unjust taxation and many who have measurably escaped all taxation will always be found opposing an honest and fair tax upon selfish grounds. . . .

. . . [It] is confidently believed that when the measure now pending becomes a law and becomes adjusted to the country and understood by the people the universal judgment will be that it equals in its satisfactory operation and excels in its justice, flexibility, and productiveness any tax law on the statute books.

The final version of the bill included an income tax with a $3,000 exemption for single people ($4,000 for married couples) and tax rates ranging from 1 to 7 percent, the highest rates applying only to incomes over $500,000. The large exemptions (by that day's standards) were intended to exempt all but the wealthiest 1 percent of the population from paying any tax at all, in Wilson's words, "in order to burden as small a number of persons [as possible]."

On March 1, 1913, the new tax went into effect. More than 40 years after the Civil War income tax was allowed to expire, there was finally another income tax.

The next 40 years of the income tax were destined to be just as stormy. From 1913 to 1954 the income tax was part of the nation's struggle for survival through war and depression. Pure tax policy questions took a back seat while the income tax was used to pursue more pressing national goals.

World Wars and Economic Collapse

By the middle of 1917, the United States had entered World War I and needed more money to pay for military operations—just as it had in the Civil War. By the time World War I was over, three separate tax bills had increased tax rates set in 1913 by nearly tenfold and the personal exemptions had dropped significantly, although 92 percent of the population still paid no income taxes at all. The first bill in 1916 became a referendum on Wilson's foreign policy of preparedness and passed 42–16 in the Senate and 238–142 in the House. The disputes in the bills of 1917 and 1918 occurred over which income classes and regions of the country should bear the burden of the tax, not whether taxes should be raised. The financial needs of the War were evident to all and not one member of the Senate or House voted against the 1918 bill.

The end of the war reduced the need for government revenues. President Warren G. Harding's Secretary of Treasury, Andrew Mellon, was an apostle of tax reduction in the cause of economic growth. He argued persuasively that high tax rates discouraged saving, drove private capital into public tax-exempt securities, and stifled work:

> Any man of energy and initiative in this country can get what he wants out of life. But when that initiative is crippled by legislation or by a tax system which denies him the right to receive a reasonable share of his earnings, then he will no longer exert himself and the country will be deprived of the energy on which its continued greatness depends. . . . On the other hand, a decrease

of taxes causes an inspiration to trade and commerce which increases the prosperity of the country. . . .

With much of the population tired of war and taxes, the Mellon tax program made its way, step by step, into the law of the land. In 1921, the maximum tax rate was cut from 77 percent to 58 percent; in 1924, to 46 percent; and in 1926, to 25 percent. Starting in 1922, the tax rate on long-term capital gains (on assets held at least two years) was also cut.

Some people now credit Mellon and his strategy of big tax cuts for the economic boom of the 1920s. A booming stock market, with only trivial taxes on the apparently certain profits, gave everyone a chance to make a fortune, or even in the rare event that the investment went sour, the loss could be written off against the investor's other income. Soon almost everyone with any spare cash had joined in, and many people had their shirts riding on the market. The get-rich-quick mood pervaded the air. As historian Frederick Lewis Allen described it later:

The speculative fever was infecting the whole country. Stories of fortunes made overnight were on everybody's lips. One financial commentator reported that his doctor found patients talking about the market to the exclusion of everything else and that his barber was punctuating with the hot towel more than one account of the prospects of Montgomery Ward. Wives were asking their husbands why they were so slow, why they weren't getting in on all this, only to hear that their husbands had bought a hundred shares of American Linseed that very morning. Brokers' branch offices were jammed with crowds of men and women watching the shining transparency on which the moving message of the ticker tape was written; whether or not one held so much as a share of stock, there was a thrill in seeing the news. . . . Thousands speculated—and won, too—without the slightest knowledge of the company upon whose fortunes they were relying, like the people who bought Seaboard Air Line under the impression that it was an aviation stock. Grocers, motormen, plumbers, seamstresses, and speakeasy waiters were in the market.

Behind this frenzy of speculation, however, stood a shaky financial structure:

Even the professional analyst of financial properties was sometimes bewildered when he found Company A holding a 20 percent interest in Company B, and B an interest in C, while C in turn invested in A, and D held shares in each of the others. But few investors seemed to care about actual worth. . . .

Meanwhile investment trusts multiplied like locusts. There were now said to be nearly five hundred of them, with a total paid in capital of some three billions and with holdings of stocks— many of them purchased at the current high prices—amounting to something like two billions. These trusts ranged all the way from honestly and intelligently managed companies to wildly speculative concerns launched by ignorant or venal promoters. Some of them, it has been said, were so capitalized that they could not even pay their preferred dividends out of income from the securities they held, but must rely almost completely upon the hope of profits. Other investment trusts, it must be admitted, served from time to time the convenient purpose of absorbing securities which the bankers who controlled them might have difficulty selling in the open market. Reprehensible, you say? Of course, but it was so easy! One could indulge in all manner of dubious financial practices with an unruffled conscience so long as prices rose. The Big Bull Market covered a multitude of sins.

It was inevitable that some economic reversal would break the bubble, and when it came in 1929–31—a loss of confidence, margin calls that could not be met, stock prices dropping, financial failures abroad and at home, rising unemployment and protectionist tariff wars—all of that speculation was as worthless as a chain letter in the hands of the first sober man in town. The big tax cuts that helped to start the boom didn't help at all when it was time for the bust.

In 1932, as the Great Depression took hold, President Herbert Hoover raised taxes in a vain attempt to balance the federal budget. The highest tax rate was increased from 25 to 63 percent, and the personal exemptions were cut. Further, there were many new and increased excise and sales taxes, and the corporation income tax and the estate tax were both increased. But the economy was too weak to provide enough revenues to balance the budget, and in fact taxes, by taking money out of people's pockets, made matters worse.

President Franklin D. Roosevelt continued the trend toward higher taxation in two tax bills, passed in 1934 and 1935. The 1934 bill focused mostly on problems of tax avoidance through loopholes in the tax law. The treatment of capital gains was changed so that it no longer favored those with the highest incomes, and gave less relief to those with capital losses. The 1935 act, on the other hand, concentrated much more on tax rates. It reduced taxes for those with relatively low incomes while raising taxes for those at the upper income levels. Roosevelt used tax policy to attack what he called "economic royalists."

Despite scathing opposition, Roosevelt's proposals were accepted because most people believed the fortunate should provide more revenues to help care for those whose luck had run out in the Depression. New programs, including Social Security and unemployment compensation, changed our ideas of what government should be. Taxes would now be spent not just for defense but human needs as well.

The outbreak of World War II put millions of Americans back to work, and once again, national survival demanded increased federal revenue. Before the war was over, the maximum tax rates exceeded 90 percent, and the personal exemptions were reduced so much that almost 75 percent of the population had to pay income taxes. In effect, World War II changed the federal income tax from a "class tax," applicable only to the most well-off, into a "mass tax."

Americans enjoyed some brief tax relief in the late 1940s, but when the United States became involved in the Korean War, the maximum tax rate rose again to over 90 percent, and the lowest tax rate was increased to over 20 percent.

Today's Tax Law

By the end of the fighting in Korea, however, the income tax law was in a state of confusion. For 20 years the law had been the subject of almost constant emergency legislative action while most of the nation's attention was focused elsewhere. President Eisenhower declared: "Our whole system of taxation needs revision and overhauling. It has grown haphazardly over many years. The tax system should be completely revised."

So the President and the Congress cooperated in writing a new tax law. The product contained no dramatic departures from the old law; it merely removed some anomalous provisions and internal inconsistencies, while performing the important task of reorganizing the law itself so that it was easier to understand. The result was the Internal Revenue Code of 1954, which is still the heart of our current income tax law. It was also the beginning of the slow downhill slide to today's complicated and inefficient income tax.

How the Income Tax Went Wrong

The 1954 law preserved wartime tax burdens in peacetime. The rates ran from 20 percent on the smallest taxable incomes to 91 percent on the highest, and the exemptions were small enough to make more than half the population pay at least some tax.

There were no large tax cuts for two big reasons. First and most important the "cold war" against Communism continued even though the "hot wars" had ended. For the first time in our history, the United States was maintaining a fully prepared military establishment in peacetime. To finance that national defense took more tax dollars.

The second reason was that the federal government maintained commitments to unemployment insurance and other programs that were first undertaken during the Great Depression.

There was no "tax revolt"; most people accepted the heavy tax load. But before long, powerful people were coming to Washington asking quietly for "tax breaks" for specific groups or interests.

These tax "breaks" or "preferences" came to be known as "tax expenditures," because if the government declines to tax part of someone's income to encourage him to grow timber, look for oil, or whatever, it is really as if the government were *spending* money to pay that person to do the same thing.

As these tax expenditures or "loopholes" in the law grew in number, they began to cause problems.

For one thing, they forced the IRS to use more forms, with more lines, and pages and pages of new instructions—confusing the average, intelligent, honest taxpayer. On the other hand, clever taxpayers found that they could use the many special provisions to avoid paying their fair share of tax. Meanwhile, large tax expenditures were going unnoticed (and remaining in effect for years) while much smaller government spending programs were being scrutinized carefully by Congress. In addition, these tax expenditures encouraged investors to go into tax-preferred lines of business, often generating excess investment there and too little in other areas.

The biggest problem was that the growth of tax expenditures *narrowed the tax base*. In other words, we wound up with less income to tax. And because we need to collect a certain amount of revenue year after year, we had to impose high tax rates on the income still subject to taxation.

High tax rates have lots of ill effects, as I've pointed out earlier. The higher the tax rates, the less any taxpayer gets to keep from extra work or saving. By all accounts, many workers today don't feel that overtime is worth the bother; the IRS takes so much of the extra money, the paycheck hardly seems any different. Other people don't see much point in saving, because the taxes on the interest are so high; that is part of the reason why we have fallen behind in modernizing our industrial base.

High tax rates also make cheating the IRS a high-paying job. When the average taxpayer might pocket $35 by claiming a false $100 contribution to charity, one might wonder whether the system is offering too much of a temptation. A growing number of people are avoiding the tax system entirely. They are going "underground," taking their pay in cash and not reporting all or most of it. This "underground economy" costs the Treasury billions, and costs many Americans their respect for their tax system and their government. And the problem seems to be growing; the most recent estimates are as much as $100 billion in revenues lost in 1983.

For all their other problems, high tax rates feed on themselves. The higher the tax rates, the greater the incentive to persuade Congress to give your business or industry its very own tax expenditure. And that is what many special interest groups have done, year after year. These new tax breaks further narrow the tax base, which further raises the required tax rates, which induces still more people to ask for special relief—and so on.

The easiest potential escape from this vicious circle is economic growth. When taxpayers' incomes increase, they move up into the progressive income tax's higher tax rate brackets, and so the government's revenue increases even faster than the people's incomes. If this additional revenue is used to finance tax rate cuts, the incentive to use and lobby for tax loopholes can be reduced. It might even be possible to gather the political strength to repeal some of the tax loopholes and reduce rates even more. That kind of tax restructuring would achieve several important objectives: simplification of the income tax, fairer treatment of taxpayers in different circumstances, and increased incentives for the most productive forms of economic activity.

Unfortunately, the income tax was allowed to continue in its complex, high-rate form through the 1950s even though economic growth (and some inflation) might have allowed rate reduction and some simplification.

But President John F. Kennedy recognized the cost of a tax code riddled with loopholes in 1962. He proposed an income tax cut designed to spur a sluggish economy into faster economic growth and prosperity, even though the federal budget was already in deficit. Under his plan, the individual tax rate schedule would drop from a range of 20 to 91 percent to a 14 to 65 percent range. It was this innovative use of fiscal policy that stirred controversy and got headlines. But as part of his tax package, President Kennedy also proposed closing numerous loopholes to make the tax system simpler and more fair:

> My tax proposals include substantial permanent reductions in individual and corporation income tax rates as well as a number of important structural changes designed to encourage economic growth, increase the equity of our tax system, and simplify our tax laws and administration. . . . The recommendations . . . provide for more equitable tax treatment through changes affecting the tax base and remove certain tax concessions that will no longer be appropriate. In every respect, the proposals are consistent with generally accepted

American standards of fair play, while at the same time they are designed to provide needed economic incentives.

President Kennedy proposed to cut back sharply on itemized deductions, to add back some special exclusions of income into the tax base, and to repeal a special tax credit for corporate dividends. Unfortunately, the economic policy of stimulating growth through lowering tax rates and eliminating loopholes—the heart of the Kennedy proposal—proved so controversial that the President was forced to compromise. The compromise was to omit the loophole—closing part of the package. Of course, this meant that additional tax revenues were lost, and so tax rates could not be reduced as much. Instead of getting the top rate down to 65 percent, he had to settle for a top marginal rate of 70 percent as well as rates higher than he had initially proposed for 25 of the 27 tax brackets. Every income level lost because Congress would not take on the special interests and close a few loopholes.

The problem of high tax rates and tax expenditures feeding on each other continued. The complexity of the 1954 tax law persisted and grew, and an opportunity to capitalize on the unprecedented economic growth of the 1960s to create a simpler and more efficient tax system was lost.

Even with only part of his tax program adopted, President Kennedy's overall economic policy proved to be a success; the United States began its longest period of continuous economic growth on record. What level of prosperity we might have reached with bigger rate reductions, we'll never know. But the inflation of the Vietnam War soon set in. With more money in people's hands and defense expenditures for

Vietnam increasing, it was only a matter of time until we all had to pay the price of higher inflation. If, on the other hand, we had paid for defense increases or the tax-rate cuts with loophole closings, inflation would not have been so strong. One final irony is that by the late 60s much of the Kennedy-Johnson tax cut had been undone by inflation pushing people into higher tax brackets.

The federal government began to keep track of its many tax expenditures in 1967. In that year, 50 were counted, and they cost the government $37 billion in uncollected revenues—compared to about $95 billion of actual revenues. But even when those statistics were published for everyone to see, the high tax rates continued to encourage the creation of more and bigger tax expenditures. By 1974, 71 tax expenditures were costing the federal government about $82 billion in uncollected revenues—about half of the actual revenues of $162 billion.

For unexpected reasons, 1974 was an important year for tax policy—Congress passed a law creating a new budget process. Until then, Congress acted on each part of the federal budget piece by piece, and no one checked the total amount of money to be spent. Needless to say, spending tended to get out of control.

Under the new budget process, Congress had to decide before each fiscal year how much money it would spend, in total and within each of several categories. As a result, new spending proposals were examined much more closely to prevent breaking the spending limit of the budget.

But because inflation kept pushing taxpayers into higher brackets, government had more revenue. With that cushion, it was easier than ever to create new loopholes without causing tax revenues to fall short of their target. So instead of creating new spending programs, or instead of giving tax cuts, Congress promoted many of its favorite causes through the tax side of the ledger—by telling people that if they did what Congress wanted them to do, they would pay less tax.

By 1981, despite a major attack on tax loopholes by President Jimmy Carter, the number of tax expenditures had grown to 104, costing about $229 billion in lost revenue—almost two-thirds as much as total actual revenues and about one-third of total actual spending.

During his campaign in 1980, President Reagan made tax policy the major part of his economic program. He appealed to the angry middle class that had seen its living standards decline and its salary raises eaten up through bracket creep. But his response to the high tax rate/tax expenditure problem was incomplete and unbalanced. After his election Reagan proposed three years of deep tax cuts with no reduction of tax loopholes; in fact, the bill the President endorsed in the Congress created eight new tax expenditures. These new tax preferences plus the reduction of tax rates promised to cost the federal government $750 billion by 1985.

Financial markets were frightened by huge and seemingly unavoidable budget deficits in the years to come. They concluded there would not be enough credit to finance private sector growth and budget deficits. The result was sky-high real interest rates (that is, after allowing for inflation). New homes and cars became unaffordable luxuries for most families, causing near-depression conditions for the construction and automobile industries. Unemployment soared to levels unseen since the Depression. Business investment plans were reduced or cancelled. The middle class got some relief from bracket creep, but that did not increase disposable income because, at the same time, the middle-class family paid more in interest charges and lost some federal benefits.

Similar mistakes were made with the corporation income tax. The Reagan tax bill gave big corporations tax benefits that were often large enough to wipe out their entire income tax bills. And by cutting corporate tax revenues for years to come, it shifted more of the tax burden to individuals. The share of total tax revenue represented by corporate income taxes dropped from 12.5 percent in 1980 to an estimated 9.9 percent in 1984.

The Reagan program showed that it does little good—and possibly a lot of harm—if tax rates are cut dramatically while tax expenditures and loopholes are preserved. With the Reagan law fully in effect in 1984, inflation has pushed many taxpayers into brackets with rates only a percentage point or two below what they paid in 1978. People are even surer than before that the tax system is unfair, because the tax expenditures and loopholes are still there; for the same reason, the tax law is just as complicated as ever. Tax shelters abound. The underground economy of income unreported to the IRS is bigger than ever. The new tax law has done almost nothing to improve the tax system, and it has cost millions of Americans their jobs.

And here is the ultimate irony: In 1954, the income tax rates were kept at wartime levels to pay for the new defense establishment and the social programs begun during the Depression. Since 1954, our economy has enjoyed some years of unparalleled growth—making these defense and social burdens easier to bear. If we now had tax expenditures as few and as small as those in the 1954 law, we could pay our bills with 1920s-style tax rates at or below 30 percent. Instead, because of the tax loopholes demanded by so many special interests, we are left with tax rates up to 50 percent in a tax system that is complicated, inefficient, unfair, and the subject of public wrath.

There isn't a shadow of doubt that we can do better.

CHAPTER 7

BACK TO BASICS

(Principles of an Ideal Income Tax)

It is clear that the biggest problem with our income tax is the mass of tax loopholes. These special provisions complicate the forms and instructions; permit large-scale tax avoidance by those with the money, skill, and inclination; and encourage investment in tax shelters instead of enterprises that could make us more productive as a nation. We have to weed these special provisions out of the tax law. But with the law so overgrown with loopholes, who can tell the loopholes from the essentials? And how can we be sure that repealing tax preferences won't cause more pain than it will prevent? One person's loophole, after all, is another's incentive.

Before we can remove the unnecessary parts of the tax law, we have to know what the necessary parts are; we have to know what an ideal income tax would look like. But there are problems in imposing an ideal income tax on the real world. Because taxpayers have made long-term commitments on the basis of existing tax preferences, suddenly repealing every tax preference would cause hardship. The real challenge is to adapt the ideal income tax to the real world and provide for an orderly transition.

Basic Principles

We collect taxes to raise enough revenue for the nation's legitimate public purposes. If we want a strong national defense, an up-to-date highway system, loans for higher education, and grants for the arts and for medical research, we have to collect taxes for them. If they aren't worth the necessary tax effort, then they aren't worth doing. So our political process has to decide how much to spend; we have to balance the benefits of government spending against the pain of taxing ourselves.

Fiscal Year 1984 ESTIMATES OF TAX SHARES	
Individual Income	43.8%
Corporate Income	9.9
Social Security	35.7
Excises	5.7
Estate and Gift	0.9
Customs	1.4
Miscellaneous	2.6
	100.0%

Once we know how much revenue we need to collect, we have to decide how to collect it. Although an increasing amount of tax revenues comes from social security taxes, the chart above clearly shows that we collect over 50 percent of our taxes from the individual and corporate income taxes. We use an income tax because income is the best measure of *ability to pay*. We could have a simpler tax system by just dividing up the federal budget equally among every man, woman and child in the country, and sending everyone a bill for the same amount. But such a system could never win popular support, because it would be unfair and burdensome to our poorest citizens, those least able to pay. To raise revenues more fairly, we assess taxes according to the amount of income each taxpayer receives. Those who have more should pay more.

To avoid the complications, unfairness and inefficiency of the loopholes in today's tax system, we should set out to do two things in the most straightforward manner possible: measure income and tax it. Unfortunately, in a complicated economy, measuring income is not a simple task. We must allow deductions for the person who has legitimate business expenses in the course of earning his income; the net income of a mom-and-pop grocery does not include the money that pays for the light, the heat and the food on the shelves. We need to provide some protection for those with the lowest incomes; we wouldn't want to tax the first dollar of income of a family supported by a single, minimum-wage job. And we also need enforcement procedures to see that these minimum necessary provisions are not abused.

But once income is properly measured, there should be no additional tax preferences. Any further deductions or credits complicate the tax code and favor taxpayers who can take advantage of them over taxpayers who cannot. So again, the ideal policy is simply to measure income and to tax it.

Even then, how should income be taxed? A vigorous debate has recently risen between advocates of progressive taxation and those of the flat-rate income tax. The current tax law has progressive tax rates: starting in 1983, the lowest-income taxpayers pay a tax rate of 11 percent on each additional dollar of income; that tax rate increases as income rises, to a maximum of 50 percent for those with the highest incomes. Under the flat-rate tax, everyone would pay the same tax rate, probably about 19 percent, on each dollar of income.

The telling advantage of progressive taxation is its basic fairness. If low- and middle-income taxpayers buy necessities with their *last* dollars of income, but upper-income taxpayers buy luxuries, then the upper-income citizens clearly have a greater ability to pay tax; they should be taxed at a higher rate on those last dollars of income. (Or, as Senator Sherman said back in 1871, "Can a rich man with an overflowing revenue consume more sugar or coffee or tea or drink more beer or whiskey, or chew more tobacco than a poor man? You tax tobacco at the same rate per pound, whether it is tobacco for the wealthiest or the poorest." But . . . "the poor have to consume a greater proportion of their income in its purchase than the rich. . . . " So they "levied a reasonable income tax upon such incomes as are above the wants and necessities of life.") Those with the highest incomes have also benefited most from the society that taxes help to maintain; it follows that they should carry a greater share of the load. Most Americans feel if you've succeeded individually, then you should give a little more back to the national community than if you are struggling from paycheck to paycheck.

If we were to change from our present progressive tax system to a flat-rate system, most middle-income taxpayers would have their taxes increased, while the main beneficiaries would be the wealthy who need help the least.

Some people argue that a progressive income tax stifles initiative by imposing excessive taxes on those who earn high incomes, and that it encourages the government to raise only the top tax rates on the rich whenever more revenue is needed. Presidential counselor Edwin Meese even went so far as to call the progressive income tax "immoral" because, in his view, "it penalizes [people who are] successful." But this reasoning doesn't square with our recent experience or with the principles of an ideal income tax. Eliminating the many tax preferences and loopholes will allow the highest tax rates to be reduced drastically—so there will no longer be any question of high rates stifling initiative.

Besides, the American people are fair-minded; they don't want to over-tax either the poor or the rich. The 1981 tax law demonstrated clearly that many Americans are concerned about the tax treatment of the wealthy—probably because they hope to be wealthy someday themselves. No one wants to "soak the rich" if he hopes to be rich one day and does not want to be "soaked" in turn. Such dreams of future success are a powerful driving force in our entrepreneurial economy. As a teammate once said to me, "In America anyone can become a millionaire. Don't have to be true, but as long as people believe it, it's true." (By the way, I think he became one.) These dreams should be nurtured, not destroyed, and the path to their attainment should be made clearer with low tax rates, rather than obscured through the use of mysterious tax gimmicks.

So the basic principles of an ideal income tax are merely these: to measure income, and then tax it as fairly and as simply as possible. While this prescription might seem oversimplified, in fact it speaks directly to the major goals of the income tax.

Ultimately, of course, we simply have to make a collective decision as to what tax rates on low- and high-income people would be fair and economically efficient. Making that decision in concrete terms is obviously more difficult than discussing it in the abstract.

Another kind of tax system is called an expenditure tax, or consumption tax. The expenditure tax, which has been highly praised in a number of leaks and unattributed remarks from the Reagan Administration, is somewhat like an income tax. The difference is that taxpayers would get a deduction for all the money they save, and would have to pay tax on all the money they borrow (or withdraw from savings); the reason for this is to encourage people to save and discourage them from borrowing. But like the flat tax, the expenditure tax is fundamentally unfair.

As Senator Sherman said, " . . . if you leave your system of taxation to rest solely upon consumption, without any tax upon property or income, you do make an unjust system." The expenditure tax says that a family with a $15,000 income that has to spend all its income to try to live decently has to pay tax on all of that income, but another family with $150,000 that can live well spending $75,000 need pay tax on only half of its income. The expenditure tax would also put a heavier burden on people whose incomes were reduced by unemployment, or illness, or other uncontrollable factors; if they borrow (or even just withdraw from their own savings) to meet their bills, they would have to pay tax on that money. Finally, the expenditure tax would give a tremendous advantage to those who had already accumulated substantial wealth. In contrast, an income tax with low rates can be fair and provide strong incentives to taxpayers with high and low incomes.

The Basic Principles and the Goals of the Income Tax

Today's tax system is complex, inefficient, and unfair. A tax system that followed our basic principles would score much better on all those grounds.

The ideal tax system would be simple because it would have no deductions, exclusions, or credits that are unnecessary for the measurement of income. The forms would be shorter and fewer in number, and the instructions to the forms would be correspondingly shorter. The average taxpayer could understand the tax system better, and would have less need to seek professional help.

The ideal tax system would also promote economic efficiency. If there were no tax preferences, people would invest to make money in the marketplace, not to lose money on their tax returns. With no tax loopholes, more income would be taxed and tax rates could therefore be reduced. This would increase incentives for work, saving, and investment.

The ideal tax system would also be fairer than the current law. Taxpayers with the same income would pay about the same amount of tax. There would be no opportunities to avoid tax through tax shelters or other abuses of the tax law. Finally, an ideal tax would relieve the lowest-income persons of the burden of taxation; taxpayers with very high incomes would pay higher tax rates than those with lower incomes, but all tax rates would be much lower than they are now. No one would be "soaked" under the ideal tax, but everyone would pay his or her fair share.

So the ideal tax, following basic principles, would correct the three major failings of the current income tax.

Problems of an Ideal Tax in the Real World

The ideal tax is clearly a winner on paper, but the translation to the real world is likely to be quite difficult. We do not have an ideal income tax now, everyone agrees; and people have been making long-range economic decisions for many years on the basis of the tax incentives actually in the law. A conspicuous example is the typical homeowner. Some people argue that an ideal tax should not allow deductions for mortgage interest and property taxes. But with millions of taxpayers locked into long-term mortgage commitments, made with the expectation of a deduction for interest and taxes, simply eliminating those deductions would cause serious pain. Homeowners' taxes would go up and the values of their homes would fall, but their mortgage payments would not change. If the tax increase squeezed them hard enough that they needed to sell their homes, they would lose money in the process. Eliminating the homeowner's tax deductions is not a step to be taken lightly.

Yet, if we carry the subsidy of real estate—even home ownership—to an extreme, we end up with a society that is housed well, but goes to work in deteriorating factories over roads and rails that need serious repair. In the ultimate sense, it is a tradeoff between today and tomorrow, between consumption desires and investment requirements, between individual pursuits and community betterment. The ideal tax system not only balances investment and consumption, but also remains neutral among types of investments.

Another problem area with the ideal income tax is the deduction for charitable contributions. Adopting an income tax completely free of special features would eliminate the current tax incentive for giving to religious, educational, cultural, and other nonprofit organizations. An important inducement to socially valuable behavior would be gone, and the charitable organizations would almost certainly be left with fewer funds on which to operate. Like the mortgage interest deduction, the charitable contributions deduction cannot be dropped casually from the tax law.

Further, the combined effects of all of the special provisions in the current tax law must be considered in building any new tax for the real world. Some taxpayers now make use of many tax loopholes in a carefully planned way to pay very little tax, and for such people a raise in taxes is of little concern. But the average American family files a tax return claiming moderate amounts of deductions for mortgage interest, charitable contributions, and other expenses. If a real world tax system is constructed, it must prevent the average family from bearing a greater share of the total tax burden. The tax rates must be carefully chosen to protect the average taxpayer.

This is why the ideal tax designed for the real world would have progressive tax rates rather than a flat-tax rate; under a flat tax, the average family would pay substantially more in tax than it does now. And those who have benefited from our economic and political system should pay more in tax than those struggling from paycheck to paycheck.

The bottom line is that a tax in the real world, unlike

an ideal tax in the abstract, has to deal with tradeoffs. We could make the income tax simpler and more efficient by eliminating commonly used deductions and cutting back on relief for low-income taxpayers, but such simplicity and efficiency could only be bought at the cost of reduced fairness, with higher taxes for lower- and middle-income groups. So moving from the drawing board into practice is less a question of attaining perfection than of balancing conflicting objectives to achieve the best overall results.

Clearly, however, we cannot have dramatically lower rates and keep all the loopholes in the present law. For every loophole that remains, the tax rates must be that much higher to fund the functions of government. There is no ideal once any loophole is allowed, just a series of tradeoffs and tough choices. If our goals are simplicity, fairness, and efficiency, the question should be what promotes the general interest, not what rewards the special interests.

Making the Ideal into the Real

The Fair Tax—The Bradley-Gephardt Bill—is an attempt to make those tough choices. We have tried to simplify the Code, eliminate the loopholes that permit tax avoidance and tax shelters, and reduce tax rates substantially—while at the same time leaving the average taxpayer better off than he is now, and seeing to it that those with higher incomes really pay a fair share. Seventy percent of the 100 million taxpayers will get a tax cut under the Fair Tax, and 30 percent will be paying more. In the next chapter, I'd like to tell you exactly what the Fair Tax does, and show you how it would help our tax system, our economy, and you.

CHAPTER 8

THE FAIR TAX

(How It Will Work)

Every elected official in history must have wished that he could give all of his constituents something without taking anything from anyone. Come to think of it, some political candidates regularly promise to do just that.

The Fair Tax isn't a free lunch. The essence of the Fair Tax is low tax rates, much lower than under the current tax law; and we can't just cut tax rates without losing a lot of revenue. Reaganomics proved that.

Despite all the talk about the Reagan tax cuts raising revenue, we now have the prospect of huge budget deficits throughout the foreseeable future. The three years after the tax cut saw cumulative deficits of about $490 billion, and there are plenty more on the way. The Congress tried in 1982 to recover some of the lost revenue by closing loopholes, but by that time it was too late; the financial markets were already in disarray, and the recession had begun. It was difficult to muster a political majority to raise taxes, even if it would make the tax system fairer; and so the loophole closing didn't go far enough.

If there is anything we should learn from the mistakes of Reaganomics, it is that the tax rate cuts and loophole closing must occur simultaneously. That way, we can maintain tax revenues at the necessary level, to keep the government's budgetary house in order; and we can give those taxpayers who lose their tax loopholes some compensation in the form of lower tax rates.

So the Fair Tax takes this lesson, and joins loophole closing and tax rate reduction in one package. But the Fair Tax includes big tax rate cuts, bigger than the Kennedy-Johnson tax cuts of 1964 and much bigger than the Reagan-Kemp-Roth tax cuts of a few years ago. They are almost as big as the Mellon cuts of the 1920s. And to cut tax rates a lot, you need to cut out a lot of loopholes. To be honest, most taxpayers will feel the loss of one tax benefit or another.

What's in It for You

So why should you give up a tax loophole? If you are like most taxpayers, you feel that the system is taking you for a ride. Why should you lose anything you've got going for you? What could be in it for you?

Well, if you want the big tax rate cuts, you *must* give up some loopholes. Remember, there's no free lunch. And if you think about it, some of our loopholes are rather silly.

Consider one tax deduction the Fair Tax gets rid of: the itemized deduction for state sales taxes. Every year, over 95 percent of the taxpayers who itemize their deductions run their fingers along two pages of tables in fine print in their tax return instruction books to find out how much they may itemize for state sales taxes. The numbers don't vary much from one category of taxpayer to another, and the amounts aren't very large, either; the deduction averages about 1 percent of income.

Of course, the tables can't be right for everybody; not every $21,000-per-year family of four in Idaho paid exactly the same sales tax, as the table blindly asserts. In fact, some people say that the tables are usually low. So as April 15th approaches, millions of American families spend their spare time adding up all of their cash register receipts for the previous year, assuming they went to the trouble of keeping them, in order to justify a higher deduction to the IRS. Can you imagine all those people, punching their pocket calculators with hundreds of numbers from tiny slips of paper? It sounds like a fifth-grade punishment.

And when all this is done, 95 percent of all itemizers still claim the deduction, and it still averages about 1 percent of income, with little variation from tax return to tax return. Yet the deduction costs the federal treasury about $5 billion per year, and that figure is growing rapidly. We have to make up that revenue somehow, and so, implicitly, tax rates have to be higher. It is those high tax rates that make many American workers turn down overtime—the extra taxes are so high that workers hardly see anything extra in their paychecks. And all because of a silly deduction for sales taxes—and more than a hundred other exclusions, credits, and other benefits hiding in 2,000 pages of tax law.

"Taxpayers using loopholes," a wise economist said a few years ago, "are a lot like a crowd of people standing tiptoed watching a parade." They are all very uncomfortable on their toes, but no one can stand flat on his feet because he would lose his view. Yet if they all could agree to get off their toes together, they all would see just as well, and they would feel much better too.

The Fair Tax is that kind of a common agreement—to give up tax loopholes so that all can enjoy lower tax rates.

There is another reason why you would be better off without a mass of tax loopholes, and that is because the loophole game is one that the average taxpayer can never win. Only a select few have the time and the money to lay out their views and ask for special tax provisions before Congress. The average taxpayer doesn't have that kind of lobbying force, nor can he rearrange his financial affairs to take advantage of the complex provisions in the tax law.

For example, do you have a foreign commodity futures trading corporation that you can use to exercise tax straddles that are now illegal in the United States? Or can you use low interest rate tax-exempt industrial development bonds to expand a business? These are both loopholes that Congress tried to close—unsuccessfully—in the last days of the 1983 session. If we don't deal with these loopholes in the basic structure of the law—and that means closing just about every loophole—we will never close them one by one.

One last thought. The loopholes that wealthy taxpayers use are almost always economically *counterproductive*. In a high tax rate system like we have today, one extra dollar of taxable income can cost a taxpayer 50 cents of taxes; so top-bracket taxpayers want to squeeze through any available loophole—or take a chance on creating a new one. Because such big money is involved, some very bright people specialize in foreign commodity trading corporations, tax-exempt, private-purpose bonds, and a thousand similar schemes. These games pay well, but they don't do the economy much good: how many potential customers of U.S. goods in Japan or West Germany or South America want to buy tax shelters? If all that effort instead went into productive work, developing goods and services either for U.S. *or* foreign consumption, we'd all be better off.

How It Works: Tax Rates

Again, the objective of the Fair Tax is to reduce tax rates as much as possible. Every loophole repeal must be considered in light of the lower rates that the package makes possible; the pain of giving up a tax benefit can be more than offset by the lower rates that come along in the bargain. As Senator Joe Biden of Delaware said at the introduction of the Fair Tax Act of 1983, "Some of the changes proposed I could not support on an individual basis. But I can support them if they are part of a comprehensive package to restore fairness, simplicity, and economic sense to our taxing system."

So let's start with the good news. The main part of the Fair Tax Act is a simple 14 percent tax on *taxable* income. This means that you merely take your total income (what is called *adjusted gross* income in tax jargon), subtract your personal exemptions and your standard deduction (or itemized deductions, if applicable), and multiply the result by 0.14. And for about 80 percent of all taxpayers, families with total incomes under $40,000 and single persons under $25,000, that is the end of the story.

The 14 percent rate is equal to the *very lowest* tax

bracket rate before the 1981 Reagan tax cuts. While it is higher than the lowest 11 percent rate today, low-income taxpayers are still better off under the Fair Tax's 14 percent rate, because of substantial increases in the personal exemption and the standard deduction. These will be spelled out later.

So for about four out of five taxpayers, the Fair Tax is as simple as a flat tax. There is no wondering how much tax will be due on an hour of overtime, a cost of living raise, or earnings from a second job—it is exactly 14 percent. And there will be no marriage penalty and no bracket creep for taxpayers, because there are no brackets.

But a flat tax for everyone would be a bonanza for the wealthiest taxpayers. Even under the current tax law, with all its loopholes, taxpayers with over $200,000 pay an average of about 25 percent of their income in tax. (Obviously, some pay a lot more, and others pay a lot less.) A 14 percent flat tax would be Christmas on April 15 for those taxpayers. But more to the real point, it would leave the federal government short of revenue, forcing an increase in the tax rate; that would give the average taxpayer higher taxes to finance a still larger tax cut for those who are better off.

So the Fair Tax cannot stop with the 14 percent basic tax. There is also an additional tax (or "surtax") similar to the structure of the original income tax of 1913. It equals 12 percent of *adjusted gross* income between $40,000 and $65,000 for families (between $25,000 and $37,500 for single persons), and 16 percent of *adjusted gross* income above $65,000 for couples ($37,500 for single people). The surtax is paid *in addition to* the basic tax; thus, the *combined* tax rates of the Fair Tax are 14 percent (on *taxable* income under

$40,000), 12 percent (on *total* income from $40,000 to $65,000, which gives a combined rate of 26 percent), and 16 percent (on *total* income above $65,000, which gives a combined rate of 30 percent.) This 30 percent maximum rate, of course, is sharply lower than the top 50 percent rate under current law.

You might wonder why the Fair Tax has this very different pattern of a separate basic tax and surtax. The reason is that this pattern results in total tax revenue equal to that under the current tax law, *with each income group paying the same amount as it does now*. For example, the people making between $40,000–50,000 pay as a group the same percent of total income taxes as they do under current law. The Fair Tax is not a disguised redistribution scheme within income groups, however, there will be winners and losers depending on how much they have used tax gimmicks to reduce their income subject to tax. And 70 percent of the taxpayers will pay less tax.

You might also think that having the two separate taxes is more complicated than the current tax law. But it is not. Keep in mind that 80 percent of all taxpayers will not have to deal with the surtax at all, and they will find out in the simplest possible way: from the amount of their total income. For that 80 percent there is only one tax rate. Remember, also, that the surtax is on *total* income—there are no special deductions to compute.

This last point is important in another connection. The surtax is on *total* income, so deductions don't count. This means that people with high total incomes cannot avoid their fair share of income taxes by loading up on itemized deductions. The Fair Tax doesn't work that way. It also has an effect on everyone with incomes above the surtax level who itemizes deductions; this will come up again later.

How It Works: Income

The Fair Tax closes many loopholes through which income escapes tax under the current law. There are far too many such changes in the Fair Tax to describe them all in detail here. (A complete listing of the provisions of the bill is included in the Appendix to this book.) To give some idea of how these provisions work, though, I will discuss three. The first, which affects primarily middle-income taxpayers, is the exclusion for employer-paid health and life insurance premiums. The second, which affects primarily upper-income taxpayers, is the exclusion for part of long-term capital gains. The third is special tax breaks for the oil and gas industries.

When employers pay all or part of the life or health insurance premiums of their employees, the employers may deduct those costs, just like cash wages, for purposes of computing their business taxes. There is nothing wrong with that; it is part of the cost of hiring labor, and so is a legitimate business expense. But unlike cash wages, the employer-paid insurance premiums are not considered taxable income of the employee. This causes two problems.

First, it isn't fair. Consider one worker who receives generous fringe benefits of this kind—fully prepaid health, dental, and life insurance—from his employer, while another worker who gets the same cash wages receives no fringe benefits. They pay the same taxes, but the first worker is clearly better off; the second has to pay out of pocket for his medical insurance, or for the medical bills themselves. Those insurance premiums are *income* for the 43 million workers in America who benefit from them, and the tax system should recognize that. The average employer-provided health insurance in America costs $1,000 per worker and ranges from $400 per person in the retail industry to $1,600 or higher per person in some primary industries.

Second, excluding those insurance premiums from tax makes them better than cash—and so workers have been maneuvering to get more of their pay in that form. In the 20 years from 1962 to 1982, fringe benefits like life and health insurance premiums have grown from 7.5 percent of total employee compensation of corporations to 17 percent. That is a classic example of the growth of a loophole reducing the amount of income subject to tax and forcing tax rates up. And there is no end in sight for the growth of this loophole. As Henry Aaron has written,

Recently such noted corporations as TRW, PepsiCo and Texas Instruments, and such educational and research organizations as Harvard, Yale, Carnegie-Mellon, Stanford, and my own employer, the Brookings Institution, have taken a short additional step. They have offered their employees a trade. They offer to pay all the qualifying health expenses of employees, provided that the employees accept an equal salary reduction. Since the payment for health expenses is a fringe benefit, it is not subject to tax. The employee gets the same number of dollars, but saves tax on all health outlays. I am sheltering another 5 percent of my income this way. . . . The consequence of these and other provisions is a drastic reduction of taxable income, now only 48 percent of personal income. Because the tax base is so drastically narrowed, tax rates on the average must be more than 70 percent higher than they would have to be if all income (over personal exemptions and the zero-bracket amount) were subject to tax. . . . It is this realization that should give us pause as we engage in the great American winter ritual of setting up our affairs to minimize our taxes. As individuals responding to the laws that exist, we would be foolish to do otherwise. But as citizens interested in fair and efficient taxation, we should try to change the laws. For we are behaving according to a fool's golden rule: as we are shifting tax burdens unto others, they are simultaneously shifting them unto us. And only the uninformed end as losers.

I'd like to let every worker keep the exclusion for his employer-paid insurance premiums. And I'd like to cut the taxes on everybody's cash income, too. But we can't do both. We have to get tax rates down, and we have to maintain federal government revenues. So the Fair Tax repeals the exclusion for employer-paid insurance premiums, and taxes them as income under the income tax.

Clearly, we will have to do a lot of adjusting if employer-paid insurance premiums are taxable. Right now, nobody pays much attention to the insurance premiums; they are like mad money, because nobody has to pay taxes on them. Employees will have to think more carefully about how much coverage they want, and employers will have to offer more options. Both will have to search more carefully for the best values in insurance plans. These will be healthy changes, and the federal government should cooperate and encourage the process. But the real payoff is that the tax rates will come down in the bargain. For many employees their total tax bill will be less under the Fair Tax, even without the insurance premium exclusion, because the tax rates will be so low.

The second example of an income tax exclusion under current law is that for long-term capital gains. Capital gains are the profits from buying and selling assets such as stocks, bonds, commodity futures, and precious metals. If such assets are held more than one year, only 40 percent of the capital gain is taxed. (In tax jargon, there is an exclusion of 60 percent of long-term capital gains.) This means that the highest tax rate on capital gains is 20 percent (that is, 40 percent of the top ordinary tax rate of 50 percent).

Unlike employer-paid insurance premiums, which primarily benefit middle-income people, capital gains are the domain of the wealthy. In 1981, according to the most recent IRS data, taxpayers with more than $1 million of adjusted gross income received 56 percent of their total income in the form of capital gains. This far exceeds the share of capital gains in any lower-income group. This means that 56 percent of million-dollar-plus incomes is taxed at a top rate of only 20 percent. Yet a single wage-earner making a mere $24,500 a year is paying a top rate of 30 percent.

Congressmen and senators on the tax-writing committees always hear clamoring for lighter taxation of capital gains: reducing the minimum holding period for the exclusion to six months or even eliminating it entirely; or increasing the exclusion to 70, 80, 90, or even 100 percent. The people pushing these ideas do have a point; lighter taxation of capital gains does encourage investment in capital assets, which can increase productivity. And someone who holds a capital asset for a long time may find his nominal dollar gain large, but due to inflation his increase in *real* purchasing power will be small.

But there is another side to this coin. Investors in capital assets have the choice of selling their assets any time they want. They can sell some assets that have gone up and others that have gone down at the same time, so that taken together there is no gain to be taxed. Then they can simply hold other assets that have gone up in value, letting their capital gains compound themselves with no tax due at all. They can sell in some years when they happen to be in a low tax bracket, so that the tax is smaller; or they can just hold on until death, when the asset can be passed on to an heir with no income tax due at all (only an estate tax, if necessary, is paid). So our capital gains tax is really a rough-justice compromise with the investor; the investor loses on some parts of the compromise, but he does win on others.

Also, like all tax incentives, the capital gains exclusion is prone to leakage. This means that the incentive can be used by people who are not serving the purpose the incentive was intended to promote. For example, investors in businesses can make the economy more productive and competitive, but speculators in precious metals and antiques, who do nothing for our competitiveness, get the very same capital gains exclusion.

We certainly want low taxes on capital gains to encourage capital formation. In fact, in the 1981 tax bill, I offered an amendment to lower the capital gains tax to 15 percent. But we also want low taxes on wages, interest, dividends, and every other reward to productive activity. There is no obvious reason why one form of income should be favored over the others by the tax system. So the Fair Tax eliminates the capital gains exclusion as a part of the effort to get the marginal tax rate on all income as low as possible. This means that capital gains will be taxed at the same 14, 26, and 30 percent rates as all other income.

The Fair Tax's repeal of the capital gains exclusion will not slow investment or capital formation. For one thing, the highest 30 percent tax rate is not much more than the 28 percent capital gains rate that was in effect from 1979 to 1981. When the capital gains rate was cut to 28 percent, investors hailed the dawning of a new age of capital formation and growth; if 28 percent was so good, 30 percent can't be much worse. Also, while the maximum tax rate on capital gains is increasing from 20 to 30 percent, the maximum rate on interest and dividends—other important rewards for investors—is *falling* from 50 to 30 percent. The top rate on *short-term* capital gains (on assets held less than one year) also falls from 50 to 30 percent; and there is no longer any need to hold an asset for at least one year to obtain the most favorable tax treatment, so investors can trade their assets as frequently as they wish. On balance, it's a good deal for investors and investment.

Finally, the corporate income tax is at least as important as the tax on capital gains in determining the amount of business investment that takes place. I will explain a bit later how the Fair Tax revises the corporate income tax not only to reduce tax sheltering and improve the targeting of business investment, but also to increase the quantity of investment.

The third series of loopholes benefits the oil and gas industry. Like other industries of fuel and nonfuel minerals, it fares extremely well under the Internal Revenue Code. This is due primarily to two generous preferences: percentage depletion and the so-called "intangible drilling cost deduction."

The depletion allowance is to oil and gas what depreciation is to equipment. The tax law properly recognizes that capital is consumed when oil and gas or other minerals are extracted from the ground. So it provides a depletion deduction to compensate for the exhaustion of these "wasting assets" consumed in producing income.

The problem is that for many taxpayers, the amount of the deduction bears little relationship to the amount of the oil and gas produced, or even to what it cost the producer to acquire the oil and gas property. Instead, the allowance is based on an arbitrary percentage formula that often permits the taxpayer to deduct more than his income from a particular oil- or gas-producing well year after year after year. Moreover, a taxpayer can go on claiming percentage depletion indefinitely, even though he may have long since recovered the full amount of his investment in the oil and gas property. In sum, it is an outright subsidy to invest in oil and gas drilling. And its availability has spawned some of the most lucrative tax shelters going.

The other special tax break near and dear to the heart of the petroleum industry is the deduction for intangible drilling costs. These ephemeral-sounding expenditures are actually expenses incurred in developing oil and gas wells. Normally, the Internal Revenue Code says that if a taxpayer makes an expenditure to acquire or permanently improve income-producing property, he can't deduct that expenditure all in one fell swoop. Rather, he has to deduct a portion each year based on the useful life of the property involved. Not so with oil and gas development expenditures—they can be deducted immediately and in full. This special treatment, especially in combination with percentage depletion, results in inordinately generous treatment for the petroleum industry while the rest of the taxpayers are left with punitively high rates.

Employer-paid insurance, capital gains, and oil and gas are three areas where the Fair Tax makes some tough choices. These tax breaks, and most of the others, seem well-intentioned and harmless. Piled on top of one another, however, they narrow the tax base and force us to use higher tax rates to collect the revenue we need. The high rates choke off economic incentives, encourage tax gamesmanship, and leave various and sundry groups begging for *more* tax loopholes.

We must break out of this vicious cycle. The Fair Tax shows up front the loopholes that we must give up, and the lower tax rates that are our reward.

How It Works: Deductions

Besides the exclusions of some types of income, the current tax law allows deductions to provide relief for certain taxpayers. Here again, the Fair Tax makes some definite improvements and some tough choices.

Exemptions and zero bracket amount. The most basic deduction under the current law is a $1,000 exemption for every taxpayer (husband and wife are both taxpayers) and dependent (children count as dependents). The $1,000 exemption has not been changed since 1978, and inflation has greatly reduced its value since then. The Fair Tax increases the exemption for a taxpayer to $1,600; the exemption for a dependent remains at $1,000. Thus, a husband-wife family of four can claim two $1,600 taxpayer exemptions and two $1,000 dependent exemptions, for a total of $5,200 (instead of $4,000 under current law). Under the Fair Tax, that family can earn $1,200 more without paying any tax. (Single-parent families get a special $1,750 taxpayer exemption to compensate for their higher costs of living.)

A second form of relief under the current tax law is the "zero-bracket amount," or standard deduction. Even if a taxpayer does not itemize his deductions, he can claim the standard deduction and exempt that much income from tax. About two-thirds (over 60 million) of all taxpayers claim the standard deduction now. Under the current law, the standard deduction for couples is $3,400 (so a family of four with four $1,000 exemptions can earn $7,400 without paying tax). Inflation has eaten away at the standard deduction in the last few years, just as it has the exemptions.

The Fair Tax increases the $3,400 standard deduction for couples to $6,000. For single people, the deduction increases from $2,300 to $3,000. This means that families of four can earn $11,200 ($5,200 in personal exemptions plus the $6,000 standard deduction) before paying any tax, compared to $7,400 under the current tax law.

The higher personal exemptions and standard deductions under the Fair Tax will remove from the tax rolls a lot of people with low incomes. Without the Fair Tax a lot of people who are officially defined as poor would be paying income taxes. Other people just a bit better off will have their taxes significantly reduced, and even people with $15,000–20,000 incomes will benefit from a bigger standard deduction and exemption. These people were hardly helped by the 1981 tax rate cuts for people with higher incomes.

The big increase in the standard deduction will also simplify tax filing for many people. Two million taxpayers who now itemize deductions just greater than the current standard deduction will be able to claim the bigger standard deduction under the Fair Tax. They will get a larger deduction, and they won't have to go through the hassles of itemizing—keeping records and filling out forms.

Marriage Penalty

Another important effect of the Fair Tax is how it reduces the so-called "marriage penalty"—the tendency of the current tax law to increase the combined taxes of two working people who get married. One reason this happens now is because spouses, separately, can claim a $2,300 standard deduction as single taxpayers, so together their total tax-free income is $4,600; but when they marry and file jointly, they can claim only one $3,400 standard deduction. The penalty results in part from this $1,200 drop in their total standard deduction. Because the Fair Tax has a standard deduction for couples that is exactly twice that for single people ($6,000 vs. $3,000), there is no such drop. Another reason for the marriage penalty is that the couple's incomes added together push them into higher tax brackets; but the Fair Tax has many fewer brackets. Because of these structural changes, the Fair Tax has no marriage penalty whatever for couples with combined incomes under $40,000. They pay a simple 14 percent tax. Even with the "two-earner couple deduction" under the current law, a couple at the $40,000 level now has a marriage penalty of as much as $2,730. It is even higher when one considers that many eligible couples have not been claiming the two-earner deduction, perhaps because it's so complicated. (It is equal to 10 percent of the earnings of the lesser-earning spouse, with a maximum deduction of $3,000.) Above the $40,000 income level, marriage penalties under the Fair Tax are almost always lower, even though it repeals the "two-earner" deduction. (There is still some penalty because of the Fair Tax's progressive rates.) The highest marriage penalty under the

Fair Tax is $1,600; the highest under the current law, even with the special deduction, is $4,048. If you don't take advantage of the special deduction, the penalty under current law is even higher.

The present tax law *indexes the personal exemptions and zero-bracket amounts in 1985,* to keep them even with inflation. The Fair Tax does not provide for automatic indexation for four reasons. First, the Fair Tax already increases these deductions far more than would indexation. Indexation would increase these amounts by an expected 5 percent rate of inflation in 1985, but the Fair Tax increases the taxpayer exemptions by 60 percent, and the standard deductions by 30 percent for single persons and 76 percent for couples. Second, because the Fair Tax has only three tax rate brackets (and 80 percent of all taxpayers are in only the first bracket), the problem of "bracket creep" is largely eliminated by the basic structure of the tax. Third, the Congress has always cut taxes under its own discretion to compensate for inflation, and I am sure that under the Fair Tax it will continue to do so. But we will be better off structurally because the inflation dividend can be used for further rate reduction instead of more special interest loopholes. Finally, there might be a time when we will want to consider holding back on tax cuts in order to close the deficit or putting them into effect, in order to give the economy a boost.

Itemized deductions. About one-third (over 30 million) of all taxpayers now itemize their deductions, rather than claiming the standard deduction. To bring tax rates down, the Fair Tax cuts back on some of the itemized deductions.

I have already explained why the Fair Tax repeals the deduction for state and local sales taxes. It also repeals all state and local tax deductions except the income tax and property tax deductions. The income tax deduction is needed to avoid "double taxing" income; the property tax deduction is retained as part of the long-term agreement between the federal government and homeowners. The mortgage interest deduction is retained for the same reason.

The deduction for interest other than on mortgages is cut back, however. Taxpayers may claim non-mortgage interest deductions only up to the amount of their investment income. In other words, interest expense (other than mortgage interest) is deductible for purposes of both the basic tax and the surtax, but only to the extent it offsets interest income or other investment income.

The itemized deduction for medical expenses is trimmed back. Only medical care costs in excess of 10 percent of income are deductible, compared to the current law's 5 percent. The medical expense deduction is cut back because inflation in health care costs now allows for a deduction for routine as opposed to extraordinary costs. And the income tax cannot be a first line of defense against health care costs. The medical expense deduction does not help low-income people, because they seldom itemize their deductions anyway; such people are helped by the Fair Tax through the big increases in the exemptions and standard deductions. Most middle-income working people have employer-provided insurance and moderate other medical bills; they would be better off with lower tax rates and bigger exemptions than with a small medical expense deduction. For those with very large medical bills, no tax deduction can cover the financial loss fully, because a tax deduction only reduces taxes by a fraction of the expense equal to the tax rate. So a deduction for $1 of medical expenses under the Fair Tax saves the taxpayer 14 cents. The deduction under the Fair Tax still provides some relief from catastrophic medical expenses, but the only real protection from medical costs is adequate insurance, not a tax deduction.

As you have noticed, the Fair Tax keeps the most important and widely used deductions—for mortgage interest, property and income taxes, and charitable contributions. In terms of itemized deductions, the Fair Tax isn't a radical change, although some people will reduce their taxes by switching from itemized deductions to the standard deduction.

There is a change, however, in the handling of itemized deductions for all taxpayers in the surtax income range—about $40,000 for married couples, and $25,000 for single persons. As I explained earlier, the surtax is collected against *total* income, not *taxable* income, so the itemized deductions do not reduce the surtax. There are two reasons why the Fair Tax uses this arrangement.

First, on principle, I believe that above a certain income level people should have to pay a certain fraction of their income in tax, regardless of their itemized deductions, *if the tax rates are reasonable*. In the Fair Tax, the tax rates are very low, and so the separate surtax is a reasonable contribution from people to keep their government running. And as I pointed out earlier, people cannot evade the Fair Tax by piling up itemized deductions. The surtax doesn't allow them. (The only exception to this restriction of deductions from the surtax is interest expense as it applies against investment income. If a taxpayer subject to the surtax is both borrowing [and therefore paying interest] and lending [and therefore receiving interest income], his or her interest deduction should apply at the same tax rate at which the interest income is taxed. Therefore, interest expense, in amounts not greater

119

than investment income, is deductible under the surtax.)

Second, under the Fair Tax, everyone's itemized deductions count against the same 14 percent basic tax, and so everyone's deductions are worth the same amount: 14 cents on the dollar. So the Fair Tax has a different philosophy toward itemized deductions. I believe that homeownership is a good thing, and that the tax system should encourage it. But the Fair Tax deductions contribute to everyone's mortgage interest and property taxes to the same degree—14 cents on the dollar. It isn't like the current law, when a top-bracket taxpayer's mortgage interest is reimbursed by the federal government at 50 cents on the dollar, but a dollar of a low-income taxpayer's mortgage is worth as little as 11 cents. No longer will the tax system give more in reduced taxes to the wealthy than to the middle class. These "upside-down subsidies" are eliminated by the Fair Tax.

In practice, all of this works out very simply. There is no change at all for four out of five taxpayers whose incomes are below the surtax cutoffs of $40,000 for married couples and $25,000 for single people. (That is, 80 percent of all taxpayers just claim deductions and compute the basic tax at 14 percent.) Taxpayers above the surtax range simply compute the additional surtax on total income, and it's done. I'll show how in the next chapter.

So if your income is above $40,000 (or $25,000 if you are single), what's in this for you? Why should you want the Fair Tax, if your itemized deductions are worth only 14 cents on the dollar?

The answer is the same as the goal of the Fair Tax: lower tax rates. Remember that the highest tax rate under the Fair Tax is 30 percent. The highest tax rate under the current tax law is 50 percent. That is a cut of 20 percentage points, or 40 percent. The Fair Tax rates are lower in part because there is a relation between the amount of tax deductions we allow and the tax rates we must charge. If we duck the Fair Tax's horsetrade on deductions, we will be stuck with the same high tax rates we have today.

While some people are better off under a high tax rate/high tax preference system, most of us are simply bewildered and angry with the maze of IRS regulations. Once during a radio call-in show, a constituent volunteered that he supported the Fair Tax. He told me that his next door neighbor who earned about the same income as he did paid an effective tax rate of 6 percent while the caller paid 38 percent, and he continued that the neighbor thought he was stupid because he didn't take advantage of tax gimmicks. The caller went on to say he was a chemist and preferred to do what he did best in the laboratory rather than look for tax breaks. With the Fair Tax, he concluded, he would pay his fair share but could be assured that his neighbor would also.

Under the Fair Tax, 70 percent of our 100 million taxpayers will be paying less tax, and virtually every taxpayer will have a substantial reduction in his marginal tax rate—the tax he must pay on an extra dollar of income. This means that you can keep more of the extra income you earn from extra work, a promotion, or a cost-of-living raise. It means that you needn't consider tax rates so much in your next business deal. It will give you a greater incentive to work more and invest more. You will know that you will never have to pay more than 30 percent of your next dollar of income in federal income taxes. It is good for you—and good for the whole economy.

How It Works: The Bottom Line

So after all of the reengineering, what is the Fair Tax? We should probably start to answer that question with what the Fair Tax is not:

—The Fair Tax is not a traditional tax cut, even though 70 percent of all taxpayers will be paying less. It will collect the same revenue as the current tax law in its first year, with no supply-side "rosy scenario" involved. And in fact, because it ends some tax exclusions that are now shrinking the tax base and will expand in the future, the Fair Tax will collect *more* revenue than the current law in later years.

—The Fair Tax is not a redistribution scheme. It will collect the same revenue from each income group as we do now.

So the Fair Tax *is* a plan to close tax loopholes and reduce tax rates—together. It does not pander to any one group; it touches just about everyone's loopholes, and it lowers everyone's tax rates. So it increases everyone's incentives to work, invest, and save, which is good for the economy. And it determines everyone's taxes at low, fair rates, without loopholes for some people to duck their fair share, which is good for the country.

How It Works: The Corporate Income Tax

Most people probably know that we have a corporate income tax, but very few know much about it. About the only attention the corporate tax has gotten in recent years was the furor over the so-called "safe harbor leasing"—the device in the Reagan tax cuts that allowed corporations to buy and sell tax breaks. As it happens, safe harbor leasing, even though it has since been repealed, is still a good example of what is wrong with the corporate tax, and how the Fair Tax works better.

In principle, the corporate income tax should operate just like the individual income tax: you measure income, and you tax it. The problem is that corporate income is usually harder to measure than a family's income.

The reason is that corporate income is earned through investments that last more than one year. If a young entrepreneur opens a streetcorner lemonade stand, and he spends one dollar making lemonade that he sells for three dollars, his income is obviously two dollars. But if a corporation invests $1 million in a factory that earns (after other costs) $200,000 in the first year, did the corporation lose $800,000? Not if the factory can operate for nine more years before it wears out. The corporation has to be allowed to earn $1 million free of tax to recover its original investment, but not necessarily in the first year.

The proper method, in theory, is to allow tax deductions equal to the amount of the investment, spread over the *useful life* of the investment; so for the $1-million factory lasting ten years, the firm might be allowed a $100,000 deduction each year for ten years. This process is called *depreciation*. This simple procedure has one big hitch, though; over those ten years, inflation can greatly reduce the value of those $100,000 deductions, so the deductions will not yield a large enough reserve to replace the factory. A $1-million factory in 1970 could not be built for $1 million in 1980. For this reason, the deductions are usually allowed faster than over the expected life of the asset, so that they can be reinvested sooner, to earn more interest and make up for inflation. In the example above, the factory might be depreciated over six years instead of ten. This process is called *accelerated* depreciation. The more accelerated the depreciation is, the more generous it is to the investing firm, and the sooner the firm has use of the cash freed up by depreciation.

Another device in our tax law to compensate for inflation, and also to encourage firms to invest, is the investment tax credit. For most investments in machinery, firms receive a tax credit equal to 10 percent of the price. In effect, the federal government pays 10 percent of the cost of the machine, by reducing the corporation's taxes by the commensurate amount. The idea is that firms will invest more to get the tax break, and so the economy will be more productive.

As part of Reaganomics, the 1981 tax cut greatly accelerated business depreciation allowances, and in some cases increased the investment tax credit. These changes were so extremely generous that they would clearly wipe out many corporations' tax liabilities altogether. And that raised a problem: If General Motors, for example, would save a lot of cash by making an investment and collecting the generous tax breaks, but Chrysler, for example, wouldn't save any cash because they had run years of losses and so didn't owe taxes in the first place, wouldn't that encourage GM to invest and expand, and Chrysler to stagnate? And so was born safe harbor leasing—a scheme to allow the Chryslers of the economy to sell investment tax breaks they couldn't use to the GMs, who could.

In my view, there *was* a big problem. But it *wasn't* safe harbor leasing. It was the huge depreciation deductions and investment tax credits that put firms which were rebuilding, such as Chrysler, and also many new, up-and-coming firms, at a competitive disadvantage in the first place.

And, as I mentioned earlier, the depreciation formulas adopted in the 1981 tax cuts are terribly biased; they lump most machinery into one big class with the same assumed useful life, regardless of the actual useful life of the machine. This means that some investments in machinery are treated generously, but others are treated *extremely* generously. Depending on how long their equipment lasts before it wears out (according to the actual useful lives of the equipment that different industries use), some industries are taxed far more lightly than others.

The accompanying table shows what the likely corporate tax will be on the income from a typical investment in different industries. Although the corporate tax rate in the law is 46 percent, every industry would pay less than 46 percent in tax over the lifetime of its investments, because the depreciation deductions in the current tax law are overly accelerated, and thus reduce the tax paid. The overall effective tax rate for some of these industries will be even higher when income from other capital assets is taken into account. For example, the effective tax rate for services and trade is close to 40 percent. But even more troublesome from an economic efficiency point of view are the tremendous differences in tax rates among industries—ranging from 12 percent for oil extraction to 30 percent for trade. The problem is that the low tax rates in the oil industry (and other lightly taxed industries such as construction and communications) will attract investment away from the highly taxed industries. Even if the marketplace says that we need more investment in trade, services, or manufacturing by allowing those industries a higher pre-tax rate of return, investment would tend to flow toward the more lightly taxed sectors because the tax advantages are so great.

This is not to say that there is anything wrong with the oil industry, or that we need to be swimming in retail stores. But we are competing in a rapidly changing world economy. When the marketplace signals that there is an investment opportunity in some particular sector by offering a high rate of return, we can't have the tax system standing in the way—or some other nation will get there first. And because we don't know where those opportunities will turn up, we can only accept a tax system that taxes all industries the same—so that the opportunities that the marketplace offers before taxes will also be the most attractive after taxes.

TAX RATES ON TYPICAL INVESTMENTS IN DIFFERENT INDUSTRIES

Agriculture	25%
Mining	19
Oil Extraction	12
Construction	13
Manufacturing	29
Transportation	19
Communications	16
Radio and TV	19
Electric and Gas	25
Trade	30
Services	29

Source: Gregg A. Esenwein and Jane Gravelle, *Effective Tax Rates Under the Accelerated Cost Recovery System (ACRS) and the Tax Equity and Fiscal Responsibility Act of 1982 (TEFRA)*, (Congressional Research Service, Library of Congress, January 3, 1983).

An executive of a large multinational conglomerate told me in the depths of the 1982 recession that he was simply liquidating high-tax companies, buying low-tax, low-debt companies, gutting them, and moving on with a solid balance sheet. The longer-term future of those companies and workers that provided his bridge over the recession was of no interest to the fast-moving executive who 18 months later had himself moved on to another company where he would undoubtedly make the same short-term decisions, take the money and run. Such manipulation, invited by the disparity in effective corporate tax rates, hurts our efforts to keep America Number One. It is a practice not followed by most of our responsible corporate giants, but it *should be followed* by none.

These big tax breaks caused even more trouble—the usual problem of leakage of tax incentives. Lots of sharp tax shelter operators quickly saw that the tax breaks were so big that investments didn't have to *earn* money to *make* money. Since the Reagan tax cuts, tax shelters have been booming. Want to buy a few llamas? If you are in the top tax bracket, a "creative tax planner" will be glad to tell you how it will make you money—by reducing your taxes, of course. If llamas are too exotic for you, racehorses or even plain old cows will do. Or if you are into the arts, master recordings of phonograph records, master plates of collector postage stamps, or old books might be just right.

Needless to say, none of these "investments" is going to do much for our productivity or competitiveness. But they will benefit handsomely from the business tax loopholes.

Besides the problems of depreciation and the investment tax credit, there is an array of loopholes in the corporate tax code. Among the most prominent are special tax breaks for particular industries. Oil gets percentage depletion and expensing of intangible drilling costs; timber gets the capital gains exclusion for cut trees. These loopholes make both of these industries favorites with tax shelter promoters. Banks get a special deduction for prospective losses on bad debts, even if they never have to write off a loan; and so banks pay only the tiniest fraction of their net income in tax.

All of these loopholes are so valuable because we have a high tax rate/high subsidy system. For large corporations with over $100,000 in profits, the tax is virtually a straight 46 percent of taxable income. So any tax deduction for corporations saves 46 cents on the dollar. It is no wonder that the "three-martini lunch" is such a popular corporate "perk." It is a chance for the corporation to make its employees happy, at just about half price—after taxes.

The Fair Tax addresses these problems in much the same way as it attacks the high tax rate problems in the individual income tax: by closing the loopholes and lowering the rates. The Fair Tax slows the depreciation of business buildings and machinery to a rate that allows an adequate cushion for inflation somewhat more rapid than we are experiencing today (about 7 percent); and it repeals the investment tax credit. Many other corporate tax loopholes are repealed. Then the corporate tax rate is lowered to a straight 30 percent.

The Fair Tax is not a tax cut for corporations, nor does it soak corporations. It will collect the same revenues as under current law.

The lower 30 percent rate does two very positive things for the economy and the tax system. First, it is a tremendous incentive to investment and productivity.

Under the current tax law, a corporation might enjoy the big tax benefits for a new investment; but if the investment really pays off, the profits are taxed at the very high 46 percent corporate rate. Under the Fair Tax, with its 30 percent rate, there is a greater incentive to seek the investments that yield the big payoffs—and make the economy more productive and efficient.

Second, because the value of a corporate tax deduction is less, at 30 cents on the dollar, there is much less of an incentive to play the tax deductions to the hilt. Corporate executives will not spend all Fall deciding how to roll over investments so as to lower their taxes. Instead they will spend time making more money. If a firm thinks that it is productive to send an employee out for a business lunch—and it can be—that is fine. But the firm had better think carefully, because it is paying 70 percent of the price after the tax deduction, not 54 percent. The same is true of automobiles, or any other business expenditure. The low tax rate is the best incentive because it can't be "gamed." You can fake an investment by buying a llama, but you can't—don't *want* to—fake taxable income to take advantage of a low tax rate.

Under the Fair Tax, industries like petroleum, timber, and banking will be treated fairly—no better than others, but no worse. Tax shelter opportunities will be much reduced, and investors will find it more profitable to put their money into growing, productive firms than into tax gimmicks. That is what the economy needs.

A square deal with the tax law, it turns out, will be a big improvement for some of the most dynamic firms in the economy. The so-called "high-tech" sector is very heavily taxed, largely because those firms have not yet obtained their own special tax breaks, as more established industries have. We could give these firms their own tax break—but that would reduce government revenue, and take only one sector off the list of industries that are disadvantaged by the current system. Instead, by setting up a low-rate, loophole-free tax system, we not only remove the biases against the high-tech firms, but we establish the incentives to nurture the *next* growth sector—whatever it may be.

The Fair Tax also gives lower tax rates to, among others, the retail and food and fibre industries which account for over 40 million jobs in America. Small businesses, particularly those organized as partnerships, will benefit from the reduced individual income tax rates.

Finally, notice that the 30 percent corporate tax rate is precisely equal to the highest individual income tax rate. This eliminates an incentive to create "personal service corporations" that play on the tax rate differences between corporations and individuals to avoid taxes. Personal service corporations are widely used by professionals such as doctors and lawyers—and professional basketball players.

So the Fair Tax cleans up the corporate income tax, just as it does the individual income tax. With fewer loopholes and lower tax rates, it shifts the emphasis from tax minimization to profit and progress. If we put more of our energy into building better products, instead of dodging the IRS, our corporations will win battles in the marketplace, and not just in Tax Court.

Summing Up

So the Fair Tax isn't a free lunch. We can't give away big tax cuts and pretend that it won't cause deficits; that has been tried, and it doesn't work. That was the lesson of the 1981 Tax Bill. We can't cut tax rates without closing loopholes. That was the lesson of the 1982 Tax Bill.

Chances are that in reading this chapter you have found that the Fair Tax would eliminate some tax benefit that you now enjoy. But I hope that you see that the tax rate cuts would be better for you, and for the economy.

I hope that you have also seen that a tax system with lower rates and fewer preferential tax provisions is much fairer; that a tax system allowing fewer tax shelters, and with more taxpayers bearing their fair share, is more worthy of respect. After all, if the federal government cannot set fair standards in taxation, how can it uphold justice in other aspects of our national life?

I think that you have also seen that the Fair Tax bears no hidden agenda. It is all in the open, for everyone to see. It holds constant the relative tax liabilities of income groups and corporations.

Finally, with its low tax rates, the Fair Tax is open to the dynamism of the U.S. economy. It *encourages* change—because an innovator need not overcome any tax advantages of established ways of doing things.

So the Fair Tax is fairer, simpler and more efficient than the current tax law. It is better for the economy, and better for the country.

CHAPTER 9

SOME FAIR TAX EXAMPLES

The previous chapter explained how the Fair Tax works in a policy sense—which deductions or exclusions are retained or repealed, how the tax rates are chosen, and so on. In this chapter, I would like to show how the Fair Tax works in individual examples—how each taxpayer would compute his own tax, and how the taxes under the Fair Tax would compare with those under the current law.

The examples discussed in this chapter are taken from a longer list presented in a set of tables in the Appendix to this book. All of these examples are purely hypothetical, but are constructed using the latest IRS statistics to be representative of actual tax returns with the same income and family size.

Single taxpayer, $15,000 income. The first example (Single Taxpayer No. 1 in the Appendix) is a single person with $15,000 of wage or salary income, no income from any other sources, and no itemized deductions.

Under the current law, this taxpayer would report his $15,000 of income on his IRS Form 1040 and go directly to a table that would show him his tax. (The table would, in effect, make a series of computations for the taxpayer: it would deduct his $1,000 personal exemption, and run the remaining income through the tax rate brackets.) This person's tax liability would be $1,801. He or she would be in the 20 percent rate bracket, meaning that an extra dollar of income would result in 20 cents of additional taxes.

Under the Fair Tax, this person would pay tax not only on the cash income, but also on the employer's contributions toward the taxpayer's health and life insurance premiums. Assuming that the employer paid $1,200 and $150 for health and life insurance respectively, the taxpayer's adjusted gross income would be $16,350 rather than $15,000. (The taxpayer's W2 form from his employer would report these amounts and add them up for him.)

The taxpayer would be able to take his $16,350 income to a set of tax tables to find his liability, just as under the current tax law. But assuming that the taxpayer wanted to compute his own tax liability, it would go like this:

$$
\begin{array}{rl}
\$\ 16{,}350 & \text{(income)} \\
-\ 1{,}600 & \text{(exemption)} \\
-\ 3{,}000 & \text{(standard deduction)} \\
\hline
\$\ 11{,}750 & \text{(taxable income)} \\
\times\ .14 & \text{(basic tax rate)} \\
\hline
\$\ 1{,}645 & \text{(tax)}
\end{array}
$$

Notice three things. *First,* for this single taxpayer with an income below $25,000, the surtax does not apply, and so the tax is a simple 14 percent of taxable income. *Second,* even though the Fair Tax broadens the tax base to include the $1,350 of employer contributions for insurance, this taxpayer receives a $156 tax cut. And *third,* under the Fair Tax, this taxpayer is in the 14 percent tax bracket, so the extra tax on a dollar of extra income would be 14 cents, not 20 cents. In fact, this taxpayer could earn $8,650 more still subject to the 14 percent basic tax only; *under the current law,* another $8,650 of income would put this taxpayer through the 23 percent bracket and into the 26 percent bracket.

So if this taxpayer can take a number reported to him by his employer and look up his tax in a table under the current tax law, and does the same thing under the Fair Tax, how much of a simplification is it? The answer would come best from a similar real-world taxpayer. Odds are that he would tell you that the tax system today is *very* complicated. But it isn't complicated in the tax provisions that he *uses,* but rather in the provisions that he *doesn't use.* Such a taxpayer is probably confused and angered by the thick book of tax return instructions that do not apply to him and that he cannot understand, but that he knows are saving someone else taxes. Why should the tax system be complicated in this way? This taxpayer would know that the Fair Tax has no hidden complications to benefit a select few.

Family of four, $30,000 income. A second example would be a family of four with a $30,000 income (Married Taxpayer No. 3 in the Appendix). This hypothetical family is assumed to use a number of the tax benefits in the current tax law, as a test of the Fair Tax. First, its wage or salary income is split between the two spouses, with the lesser-earning spouse making $10,000; so the family gets a $1,000 two-earner tax deduction (equal to 10 percent of the lesser-earning spouse's wages or salary). Also, the family is assumed to spend $2,000 on child care, so it receives a 20 percent child care credit. Finally, the family itemizes its deductions, in amounts typical of its income level: $3,000 of mortgage interest (average annual mortgage nationwide on existing homes is about $7,400); $1,000 of property taxes (average annual property taxes nationwide is about $1,400 per tax return); $400 of sales taxes; $1,000 of state income taxes; and $500 of charitable contributions.

Under the current law this family would compute its taxes in the following manner: It would total its income ($30,000) and subtract its two-earner deduction ($1,000) to arrive at its adjusted gross income ($29,000). Then, it would tote up its itemized deductions ($5,900) and subtract the zero-bracket amount for married couples ($3,400) to arrive at its "excess itemized deductions"($2,500). Then, to find its taxable income, it would take its adjusted gross income again ($29,000) and subtract its four personal exemptions ($4,000) and its excess itemized deductions ($2,500) for taxable income of $22,500. Finally, it would look up its tax in the tax tables ($3,003), and subtract its child care credit (20 percent of $2,000, or $400), for a final tax amount of $2,603. This family is in the 22 percent tax bracket, so an extra dollar of income would increase its taxes by 22 cents.

Under the Fair Tax it is not quite so complicated. There is no two-earner deduction, and because the family's itemized deductions are less than the standard deduction of $6,000, it would not have to itemize. Instead of a separate child care credit, child care expenses are made a simple deduction under the basic tax. The family would have to pay tax on its assumed employer-paid insurance premiums of $1,200 for health insurance and $300 for life insurance, making its adjusted gross income $31,500 (which the employers would compute for the family). While there would be tax tables so that the family could look up its tax liability, I'll go through the entire computation just to show how the tax is determined:

$$
\begin{array}{rl}
\$ \ 31,500 & \text{(income)} \\
- \ \ 5,200 & \text{(exemptions)} \\
- \ \ 6,000 & \text{(standard deduction)} \\
- \ \ 2,000 & \text{(child care expenses)} \\
\hline
\$ \ 18,300 & \text{(taxable income)} \\
\times \ .14 & \text{(basic tax rate)} \\
\hline
\$ \ \ \ 2,562 & \text{(tax liability)}
\end{array}
$$

So even with the elimination of the two-earner married couple deduction, this family would get a $41 tax cut. Further, notice that this family pays only the 14 percent basic tax, so an extra dollar of income would add only 14 cents to the family's tax bill, in contrast to the 22 cents under the current tax law. The family could earn $8,500 more at the 14 percent basic tax rate before becoming subject to the surtax under the Fair Tax (which would put it into the 26 percent bracket); if the family earns $8,500 more under the current law, it will pass through the 25 percent bracket and up into the 28 percent bracket.

Family of four, $120,000 income. To show how tax returns with higher incomes would be handled under the Fair Tax, this example is a family of four with $120,000 of total income (Married Taxpayer No. 5 in the Appendix).

Under the current tax law this family uses a number of tax benefits. The two spouses are assumed to have salaries of $40,000 and $20,000, giving them a two-earner couple deduction of $2,000 (again, 10 percent of the lesser-earning spouse's salary). Of their income,

$40,000 is a long-term capital gain, so they claim a $24,000 capital gains exclusion (60 percent of the gain). They receive another $20,000 of income from interest and dividends, and so they receive a $200 dividend exclusion (a special deduction for the first $200 of dividends). Their adjusted gross income (the sum of their receipts less the capital gains exclusion, the dividend exclusion, and their two-earner couple deduction), is $93,800.

This family also itemizes its deductions: $5,000 of mortgage interest; $5,000 of other interest; $3,000 of property taxes; $1,200 of sales taxes; $7,000 of state income taxes; and $5,000 of charitable contributions. This total of $26,200 of itemized deductions, less the $3,400 zero-bracket amount, yields $22,800 of excess itemized deductions.

To compute its taxes, the family takes its $93,800 of adjusted gross income, subtracts its $4,000 of exemptions and its $22,800 of excess itemized deductions, to arrive at $67,000 of taxable income. Its tax, from the tax rate schedules, is $18,108. Deducting an $800 tax credit for child care expenses (20 percent of an assumed $4,000 of expenses) leaves a final tax liability of $17,308. This family is in the 42 percent tax bracket, so an extra dollar of income would raise its taxes by 42 cents (unless the income was long-term capital gain, in which case the tax would be 16.8 cents).

Under the Fair Tax for this family it would be quite different. First, there would be no capital gains exclusion, dividend exclusion, or two-earner deduction. Second, the family would have to pay tax on employer contributions for life and health insurance, assumed here to be $600 and $1,200 respectively. With these changes, the family's adjusted gross income would be $121,800, instead of $93,800. Third, the family's $1,200 itemized deduction for sales taxes would not be allowed. Fourth, the child care expenses would be deductible against the basic tax, rather than creditable at 20 percent.

The family's basic tax would be computed like this:

$$
\begin{array}{rl}
\$ \ 121,800 & \text{(income)} \\
- \ \ \ \ 5,200 & \text{(exemptions)} \\
- \ \ 25,000 & \text{(itemized deductions)} \\
\underline{- \ \ \ \ 4,000} & \text{(child care expenses)} \\
87,600 & \text{(taxable income)} \\
\underline{\times \ \ \ .14} & \text{(basic tax rate)} \\
\$ \ \ \ 12,264 & \text{(basic tax liability)}
\end{array}
$$

Then, because the family's adjusted gross income is greater than $40,000, it would have to compute its surtax:

$$
\begin{array}{rl}
\$ \ \ \ 3,000 & \text{(12 percent of adjusted gross} \\
& \text{income from \$40,000 to} \\
& \text{\$65,000 (in this example,} \\
& \text{12 percent of \$25,000))} \\
7,488 & \text{(16 percent of adjusted gross} \\
& \text{income net of \$10,000} \\
& \text{interest expense over} \\
& \text{\$65,000 (in this example,} \\
\underline{\ \ \ \ \ \ \ \ \ \ } & \text{16 percent of \$46,800))} \\
\$ \ \ 10,488 & \text{(surtax liability)}
\end{array}
$$

So the family's total income tax under the Fair Tax would be:

$$
\begin{array}{rl}
\$ \ \ 12,264 & \text{(basic tax)} \\
\underline{+ \ 10,488} & \text{(surtax)} \\
\$ \ \ 22,752 & \text{(total tax)}
\end{array}
$$

So this family, even with the lower tax rates and larger exemptions under the Fair Tax, would have to pay $5,444 more. It would be in the 30 percent bracket under the Fair Tax, however, so an additional dollar of income would raise its taxes only 30 cents, instead of 42 cents under the current tax law. (An extra dollar of capital gains under the Fair Tax would also raise taxes by 30 cents, though, instead of 16.8 cents under the current tax law.)

Family of four, $60,000 income. To contrast the previous example, this family of four has just over $60,000 of income—about half as much (Married Couple No. 4 in the Appendix).

Under the current law, like the previous example, the two spouses have salaries of $40,000 and $20,000 each, and so they receive a $2,000 two-earner deduction. Unlike the preceding family, however, their only other income is $200 in dividends, which is not taxed at all because of the $200 dividend exclusion. Their adjusted gross income, therefore, is $58,000 (after the dividend exclusion and the two-earner couple deduction are subtracted from their income).

The family's itemized deductions are typical of their income level: $4,800 of mortgage interest; $2,000 of property taxes; $800 of sales taxes; $2,400 of state income taxes, and $1,500 of charitable contributions. This totals $11,500, and after deducting the $3,400 zero-bracket amount, their excess itemized deductions are $8,100.

So the family's taxable income (adjusted gross income, less $4,000 of exemptions, less the $8,100 of excess itemized deductions) is $45,900. The tax from the tax tables is $9,810; deducting a $600 child care credit (20 percent of an assumed $3,000 of child care expenses) leaves a final tax liability of $9,210. This family is in the 38 percent bracket, so an extra dollar of income would increase their taxes by 38 cents.

Notice one interesting factor here. The family in this example, with $60,200 of total income, pays 15.3 percent of its income in tax under the current tax law. The family in the preceding example, with almost twice the income at $120,000, paid only 14.4 percent of its income in tax. So the current tax law actually required a lower percentage of income tax from one family with almost twice the income of another.

Again, *under the Fair Tax* it would be quite different. It would not allow the two-earner deduction and the dividend exclusion, and it would tax the family's employer-paid health and life insurance premiums of $1,200 and $600 respectively. So this family's adjusted gross income under the Fair Tax would be $62,000. The Fair Tax would also disallow the deduction for sales taxes, so itemized deductions would fall to $10,700. And again, there would be a deduction rather than a credit for child care expenses.

So the family's basic tax liability would be:

$$
\begin{array}{rl}
\$\ 62,000 & \text{(income)} \\
-\ \ 5,200 & \text{(exemptions)} \\
-\ 10,700 & \text{(itemized deductions)} \\
\underline{-\ \ 3,000} & \text{(child care expenses)} \\
\$\ 43,100 & \text{(taxable income)} \\
\underline{\times\ .14} & \text{(basic tax rate)} \\
\$\ \ 6,034 & \text{(basic tax liability)}
\end{array}
$$

Again, because the family's adjusted gross income exceeds $40,000, the surtax is due. In this example, because the adjusted gross income is less than $65,000, the surtax is simply 12 percent of the excess of adjusted gross income over $40,000; with a $200 deduction for interest expense not in excess of investment income:

$21,800 (income in excess of $40,000)
× .12 (surtax rate)
$ 2,616 (surtax liability)

So the total tax for this family is:

$6,034 (basic tax)
2,616 (surtax)
$8,650 (total tax)

And this family is in the 26 percent bracket, so an extra dollar of income will raise this family's tax by 26 cents, compared to 38 cents under the current tax law.

Notice that this family's Fair Tax liability is about 14 percent of its Fair Tax adjusted gross income, while the family in the preceding example paid about 19 percent. So under the Fair Tax, the family with the higher income paid a greater, rather than a lesser, share of its income in tax.

So the Fair Tax is simpler to compute than the current tax law. While the Fair Tax does not reduce the federal government's total tax revenues, most taxpayers—about 70 percent—will get a tax cut. Virtually all taxpayers will be in a lower tax rate bracket, so they will have more reason to work and earn more. And when one taxpayer's tax bill is compared with another's, the result will be fairer.

That's what the Fair Tax is all about.

CHAPTER 10

THE FAIR TAX AND THE BUDGET DEFICIT

The breakdown of our federal tax system is one of the major economic problems of this decade. The huge federal budget deficit is another.

Their causes are linked. So are their solutions. And the Fair Tax can be the most important part of a plan to bring both the tax system and the budget back to health.

How Bad Is the Deficit Problem?

In a word, our deficit problem is critical. If no action is taken, the deficit will increase from about $190 billion now to about $325 billion in 1989—and there is no end in sight. Throughout this entire period, the deficits would be so large that they would absorb about half of the savings generated by the economy—savings that could otherwise finance the investment that we need for growth and productivity. The present deficit is so large that interest rates have got to stay sky high.

These high interest rates impose their own costs. They make borrowing for investment more expensive, and so will slow our rate of capital formation and our long-term growth. The deficits really are borrowing from the prosperity of our children, and their children.

The high interest rates bred by the large deficits attract foreign investment funds into the U.S. (last year foreigners bought $172 billion of U.S. Government debt); that raises the exchange rate for the dollar, which makes imports cheaper to us, and makes our exports more expensive overseas. So our businesses are made less competitive and lose sales both here and abroad, which costs us jobs. As we finance our gigantic deficits out of the savings of foreigners, we not only send tax dollars to pay them interest, but we also give them the power to pull the rug out from under our recovery. All a foreign investor must decide is that the dollar interest rate now being offered won't cover his loss in terms of his own currency when he converts dollars back to yen or marks. He then buys no more U.S. Government obligations—until the interest rate goes up to offset the decline in the dollar's value. In addition, if a foreign country raises its interest rates in a fight against imported dollar inflation, foreign capital might well flee home, leaving us with a rapidly declining currency and real upward pressures on our own interest rates, with all that means for higher unemployment and slower growth.

Further, every dollar of deficit adds to the national debt—and every dollar of the debt adds to the interest burden that we must bear in every future year. For this reason, deficits beget deficits—the deficit we run this year adds to government spending, and therefore the deficit, in every future year. At the rate we are going now, the national debt will grow faster than the economy. Already, last year, interest on the debt ($110 billion) exceeded total spending on Medicare ($81 billion). And the longer we wait to take action, the greater the accumulated national debt and interest burden become, and so the more painful the corrective action must be.

These monstrous deficits have a lot to say about another question: Was Reaganomics a success? Yes, inflation is down and that is a major achievement; and growth is up and that is reassuring. But the cost of this victory was very high in human terms—the highest unemployment since the Depression. The administration's self-administered recession left our economy weakened for the long term. The program was not balanced. Instead of just fighting inflation the policy tried to "stop and go" simultaneously, with high interest rates retarding growth while reduced taxes and big defense expenditures were stimulating growth. The result is gigantic deficits, more polarization among regions and classes, a much weakened financial system, and internationally, serious economic stresses among our allies.

And, how long can the Reagan recovery last with those huge budget deficits looming in the future? The recovery could be similar to a thin facade over the morass that lies ahead. Lots of federal government red ink continues to spur consumer spending—until the interest rates rise up to crush the recovery.

Taxes and the Deficit Problem

I spoke earlier about the three major failings of our income tax: it is unfair, inefficient, and complex, and all of these adjectives explain the breakdown of our tax system. But how has all this contributed to our deficit problem?

The first answer to this question is, "All of the above." Our complex tax system diverts highly skilled talent from productive work into complying with—and changing—and avoiding—our tax law. With more and more loopholes, there is less income actually subject to tax. As the process continues and the tax base gets narrower, incomes in the economy as a whole—and tax revenues—fall lower. Because our tax law breeds inefficiency, we have people losing money for tax reasons rather than making money; and so tax revenues are lower. And because our tax law is unfair, many honest Americans who wouldn't dream of stealing in just about any form are sorely tempted to cheat on their taxes.

This last point deserves some amplification. The IRS estimates that taxpayers are evading about $100 billion a year in income taxes.

Other experts estimate the underground economy has a gross national product as big as $600 billion; middle-of-the-road estimates are about $400 billion. If the latter number is correct, America's underground economy would be the sixth largest economy in the world—behind West Germany, France, England, the Soviet Union, and the legitimate U.S. economy.

Less than 10 percent of that total is accounted for by income earned in illegal activities, which we would probably expect to be concealed from the IRS no matter how the tax system worked; and only about another 5 percent of the total is the result of underpayment by corporations. So 85 percent of the revenue shortfall is due to individual taxpayers evading taxes on their legally acquired income.

Economists who have studied the underground economy agree that because of it, the GNP is probably

10 percent bigger than official estimates, and the labor force may be 5 percent larger. What these numbers mean is that people who are out of work might not be out of work. They might just be off the books. But no one knows for sure, so suspicion grows and more and more citizens feel alienated from government and each other.

Our tax system has always operated through voluntary compliance; taxpayers accurately reporting their own income and paying the tax that is due. That's really the only way it can operate successfully; the IRS can't possibly audit every tax return in detail to force people to comply. (A businessman I know shared a concern he has about his 24-year-old son who has just started to work for a major corporation. "All he can think about is avoiding taxes," the father said. "I'm worried that he feels no obligation to finance government." When the father told his son to stop worrying about taxes and start developing his skills, the son, attuned to hypocrisy, pointed out that the father spent a lot of time with his tax-planner.)

So if this tradition of voluntary compliance breaks down, we will have an entirely different—and far less desirable—tax system. People's tax liabilities will be based on how much they are willing to risk in the "audit lottery," not on their fair shares of the government's legitimate expenses. We will have the law of the jungle instead of the law of the land. It isn't a pretty picture.

Our present tax law is pushing us toward that unfortunate end. If people don't respect the tax system, they won't comply with it. We need to give the American people a tax system they can respect and one with which they have the prospect of closing the deficit fairly.

Some Non-Solutions for the Deficit

The deficit problem will not solve itself—we cannot "grow out of" these deficits. Given present tax law, the economy will have to grow at approximately a 6.3 percent rate in each of the next five years to close the deficits projected by the Congressional Budget Office. Last year it grew at a 6.1 percent rate. The highest five-year average growth rate since the Korean War occurred during the Kennedy-Johnson years when the economy grew at 5.4 percent. To add further perspective, there is only one year since 1951 that growth exceeded 6.3 percent (1955—6.7 percent).

The 1981 Reagan tax cuts will prevent taxes from growing fast enough to close the deficit gap. With big individual income tax-rate cuts, indexing of tax brackets, and expansion of tax loopholes, individual income tax receipts will only keep pace with the economy, not outrun it. The big Reagan tax cuts for corporations mean that corporate tax receipts also will grow only as fast as the economy and no faster. Estate tax revenues, because of the Reagan tax cuts, are failing. The Social Security system—taxes and benefits—is designed to roughly break even, not to make money. So tax receipts, considering the role of the Social Security system as a whole, will not grow enough to reduce the deficit.

That leaves spending. The Reagan Administration proposes a huge defense buildup but, similar to Lyndon Johnson in the financing of the Vietnam War, they refuse to pay for the defense increases with higher taxes. The large deficits that we are running now increase both the national debt and interest rates, so the federal government's interest bill to service the national debt is growing by leaps and bounds. By 1988, given our present deficit path, it will take $200 billion annually in interest to service the national debt. This means that we have to cut spending aggressively in the rest of the budget just to stand still—much less to make progress in reducing the deficit. In 1981 and 1982, the Congress gave President Reagan virtually everything he asked for in spending cuts. Nondefense, non-Social Security spending is now the same percentage of GNP that it was in the late 1960's and with no further changes in law, it will drop by 1986 to where it was in the early sixties. Now when we look for more ways to cut spending, it is much harder to find the waste, fraud, and abuse. And all of this is against a backdrop of a crumbling national infrastructure, a public education system in crying need of funds, and millions of decent, hardworking Americans suffering from the loss of their jobs in a changing economy. All of these problems will ultimately rest with the federal government, at least in part; many states and localities are too strapped for revenues to bear the whole load. So we can cut spending as much as we possibly can but, if we are to meet our national responsibilities, we cannot cut spending enough to close the deficit gap without help from the tax side.

The Fair Tax Is Part of the Solution

Just about everybody in the country—including such prominent Senate Republicans as Bob Dole (chairman of the tax-writing Finance Committee), Peter Domenici (chairman of the Budget Committee), and Martin S. Feldstein (President Reagan's chairman of the Council of Economic Advisers)—realize that some revenue increases will be needed to move the budget toward balance. The problem is that they propose to increase the taxes we already have. It does little good to increase an income tax that some people and corporations already successfully avoid. If the unfairness and complexity of the tax system are already driving people toward avoidance and evasion, higher tax rates (like President Reagan's proposed contingency tax) will only bring further noncompliance in the long run. And at the same time, people who already take advantage of loopholes and tax shelters to avoid paying tax won't be touched at all by a tax-rate increase. We can't increase unfair taxes. And we shouldn't waste our time imposing or increasing other taxes while our most important tax is unfair.

The Fair Tax solves that problem by putting our current tax system on a fair and economically efficient basis. It eliminates the loopholes that some people use to avoid tax. It cuts the high rates that burden those who don't avoid tax. And it lays the groundwork for improved public understanding of and compliance with the tax code.

So how does the Fair Tax help to reduce the deficit? In two ways.

First, as I mentioned earlier, the Fair Tax cuts off any number of tax loopholes that were sheltering an increasing share of income from tax. This means that even though the Fair Tax would raise the same revenues as the current law in 1985, it would raise more in later years, just because the loopholes will no longer be draining a growing proportion of revenues from the Treasury. Just as it costs more to produce 100 MX missiles than it would to produce ten, so more tax revenue is lost when 1,000 people use loopholes instead of 20 people. The longer loopholes stay in law, the more people use them, and since many are habit-forming, at higher and higher amounts, that means a greater and greater revenue loss and bigger and bigger deficits.

Second, the estimates of revenues from the Fair Tax are conservative—about $25 billion over two years. If the lower tax rates and a fairer and more understandable system bring some underground income back into the tax base, revenues will be higher. After all, once you know that you will pay only 14 cents tax on each additional dollar you earn, and that your neighbors will be doing the same, the incentive to violate the law is reduced substantially. Revenues should also be greater as tax shelter investments are redirected to earn profits in the marketplace, rather than on the tax forms. With fewer tax shelters to police and a simpler system to administer, more IRS resources will be available for enforcement, which also will pick up extra revenue. And finally, incomes and taxes will increase as the lower tax rates and more evenhanded treatment of different investments make the economy more efficient. I am not talking about a supply-side renaissance, such as the outrageous claims made for the Reagan-Kemp-Roth tax cuts; but the Fair Tax will unquestionably be better for the economy, and for tax revenues from economic growth, than were the Reagan-Kemp-Roth tax cuts.

If further progress on the deficit is necessary, other tax actions can be taken. Changes can be made in the Fair Tax that will raise more revenue but not alter the basic rate structure on the top rate. For example, if the fight against inflation continues successfully, the depreciation schedule can be adjusted so as to allow a firm to recoup their full investment in a world reflecting the actual 4 percent inflation instead of the higher 7 percent rate projected in the Fair Tax now. Second, in addition to the Fair Tax, several federal excise taxes are scheduled to decline or expire in the next five years. Those taxes could be continued at its current level. Third, substantial reductions in the estate tax from the 1981 Reagan tax cuts could be phased in over a longer period, or some of the reductions in later years could be rescinded. And fourth, before we are caught with another painful energy shortage, a reasonable tax on imported energy could encourage us all to conserve while reducing the deficit. Taking some of these steps together would increase federal revenues by about $50 billion per year by 1988. This would not eliminate the budget deficit; there would still be plenty to do in cutting spending just to get the deficit down to manageable size. But it would be a start; it would minimize the pain; and it would leave the economy better off.

Not everyone will agree with any particular plan to reduce the deficit, and we all know that raising taxes can't be fun. Indeed, some people don't agree that we need to take action to reduce the deficit. But we can agree, all of us, that we can't balance the budget by raising unfair taxes; and that if we do nothing else, the budget will move toward balance faster if we improve a tax system that now fosters noncompliance and tax sheltering. So whatever we do, the Fair Tax should be the cornerstone of a strategy to cut the deficit and improve the tax system.

CHAPTER 11

A PLAN FOR ACTION

"It sounds like a great idea, but you'll never get it passed." How many times have I heard that comment during the last two years? People are skeptical that we can break out of the stranglehold they perceive special interests to have on the tax-writing process. In fact, one political pundit put it even more starkly, "The Fair Tax will never pass," he said, "because the Special Interests are against it, and the people don't care." If he is right about the people, then he's right about the bill.

I think he is wrong. I think we can get a different tax system with fewer loopholes and lower rates for all Americans.

Some will argue that the complexity of the current system reflects the complexity of our economy, and that to seek simplification is to be oblivious to the nuances of modern America. I reject that thesis. If anything, it is the complexity of modern life that is killing our spirit, on the one hand, and pushing us to extreme solutions, on the other. The Fair Tax simplifies and clarifies how we raise revenue for government. It liberates us from the web of suspicion and inequity that covers our tax system today. It frees us to accept the challenge of the next decade in ways that stimulate innovation but do not reward sloth.

Education is the purpose of this book. I believe the more people understand the history and structure of our present tax system, the more they will call for change. If the American people, after reading and understanding the Fair Tax, don't want it, then so be it. But if they reject it because they have never heard about it or because they hear only the special interests predicting national collapse if they have to give up their loophole, then it would be a pity.

Moving toward a new tax system requires a strategy for action. It boils down to organizing the general interest against the already well-organized narrow interest. People who agree with the argument of this book must write to their representatives, contribute to candidates who espouse it, and work to organize their friends.

To begin, they can send a message to the President, the Speaker of the House of Representatives and the Majority Leader of the Senate that they are fed up with the present tax system and that they want a fairer, simpler system with lower rates. They can join the campaign for the Fair Tax by getting petitions from the Fair Tax Foundation, P.O. Box 76895, Washington, D.C. 20013, and by insuring that their friends sign and return it. It is only with the participation of the people that a new tax system will be born. Change must come from the grassroots; it must, like a mighty river, be fed by the rivulets and small streams of public opinion.

Let me remind those experts in Washington who say

that the Fair Tax has no constituency that it has more congressional cosponsors than Kemp-Roth two years before its enactment. Washington experts have not seen the disbelief in people's eyes when they learn the costs of loopholes; nor have the experts seen people's willingness to share in a solution that is fully presented, with losses lined up clearly against gains.

Some people say that our founding fathers saw the general interest as a composite of special interests shaped by the institutions of our democracy to limit excess and to assure stability. In fact, though, from the very beginning, our founding fathers reserved their highest praise for those who acted in the general interest. They believed that public virtue meant service to the community, going beyond the narrow interest of faction to the general interest of the community. The Fair Tax is the call to return to the values of our first leaders, and that is why it can't be dismissed without simultaneously diminishing our heritage. It is the right policy bridge between a past we're proud of and a future we're unsure about. It is a choice about ourselves.

APPENDIX

155

Questions and Answers

Q. How would the Fair Tax affect the withholding system?

A. The Fair Tax does not change withholding. Because 80% of taxpayers will pay a flat 14% rate, the Fair Tax will be easier to administer. There should be less under-withholding and less over-withholding than under the present system.

Q. Wouldn't there be thousands of accountants out of work?

A. Businesses will always need accountants. Accountants aren't just tax return preparers. They keep a company's books and records, prepare filings required by agencies like the SEC and help figure out a firm's profit and loss. Individuals with complex financial transactions will also need the help of accountants. What the Fair Tax will do is end the need for armies of accountants whose sole responsibility is to keep track of loopholes and help people figure out new schemes to avoid paying taxes.

Q. Would local and state governments continue to assess taxes the same way or would they adopt the Fair Tax?

A. That would be up to the states and localities. A number of states already pattern their tax systems on the federal one. Enactment of the Fair Tax would give the states an opportunity to streamline their systems and make them fairer. I imagine a lot of state legislatures would find that opportunity very attractive. In the short run, adoption of the Fair Tax would have some effect on the states because many of them use the federal tax return's adjusted gross income figure as the basis for assessing state tax liability.

Q. Won't limiting the medical deduction to expenses in excess of 10% of AGI place a hardship on large families?

A. No. The 10% threshold is per family, not per individual, so large families are more likely to meet the 10% test than small ones. Moreover, large and small families pay the same amount of premiums for health insurance. This tends to favor big families. And medical insurance, not tax deductions, must be the first line of protection from the financial cost of illness.

Q. Would the Fair Tax still permit income averaging?

A. No, it is repealed. With the Fair Tax's lower rates and fewer brackets, variations in income will have a much smaller effect on tax liabilities. The Fair Tax simplifies the entire rate system. This is preferable to having a special income averaging provision which is inordinately complicated.

Q. Would tax-free income for minors still be permitted?

A. Yes, people will still be able to set up trusts for custodial accounts for minors. However, the benefits of doing so will be much smaller because the top rate will be 30%, not 50%.

Fact Sheet on the Bradley-Gephardt "Fair Tax Act of 1983"

This legislation will make the federal income tax system simpler and fairer and the economy more efficient. It will reduce tax rates and eliminate most existing deductions, credits and exclusions. It also will raise revenues approximately equal to those collected under existing law without changing the tax burden for any income group.

Summary of Key Positions

For Individuals
—A simple, progressive tax with three rates: 14%, 26% and 30%.
—About 80% of all taxpayers will pay only the 14% rate. The 26% rate will apply only to individuals with adjusted gross incomes exceeding $25,000 and to couples with adjusted gross incomes exceeding $40,000. The top rate of 30% will apply only to individuals with adjusted gross incomes over $37,500 and couples with adjusted gross incomes over $65,000.
—An increase of the personal exemption from $1,000 to $1,600 for taxpayers and spouses ($1,800 for a single head of household) and an increase in the standard deduction from $2,300 to $3,000 for single returns and from $3,400 to $6,000 for joint returns. A family of four could earn up to $11,200 before receiving their first dollar of taxable income.
—Repeal of most itemized deductions, credits and exclusions except those generally available to most taxpayers. Retained will be the $1,000 exemptions for dependents, the elderly and the blind; deductions for home mortgage interest, charitable contributions, state and local income and real property taxes, payments to IRAs and Keogh plans and employee business expenses; ex-

158

clusion of veterans benefits, Social Security benefits for low and moderate income persons and interest on general obligation bonds. The personal exemptions and itemized deductions will apply only against the 14% rate.

For Corporations
—A tax rate of 30%.
—Repeal of most existing tax deductions, credits and exemptions that distort investment decisions.
—A new depreciation system that doesn't favor one type of asset over another.

Technical Explanation

The legislation significantly reduces tax rates and broadens the base of the individual and corporate income taxes by eliminating most tax preferences. It also smoothes out the rate schedule of the tax and sharply reduces "bracket creep" and the "marriage penalty." The changes are designed as if they were to take effect in 1985 and they are approximately revenue and distribution neutral with respect to tax liability in that year. Transition questions will require that some tax preferences be phased out gradually rather than changed abruptly. However, to establish lower rates and a broader tax base as the direction for federal tax policy, 1985 serves as the baseline date for all the analysis.

Individual income tax structure
For about 80% of individuals, the income tax is a uniform 14% tax on taxable income (the base tax). Taxable income is net after personal exemptions and either the standard deduction or the allowable itemized deductions. The personal exemptions are $1,600 per taxpayer (i.e., $1,600 on a single return and $3,200 on a joint return) and $1,000 per dependent. Single heads of households receive an exemption of $1,800. The extra exemptions for the elderly and blind continue at $1,000. The zero bracket amount (standard deduction) increases to $3,000 for single returns and $6,000

for joint returns ($3,000 for separate returns of married persons).

For upper income taxpayers, the regular 14% income tax is supplemented by an additional progressive tax (surtax) of 12% and 16% on adjusted gross income in excess of $25,000 for single returns and $40,000 for joint returns. Only about 20% of all taxpayers are subject to this surtax. The combined effect of the 14% base tax and the surtax is a top marginal tax rate of 30%.

The personal exemptions and itemized deductions retained in the Fair Tax apply only against the 14% base tax. The rate schedule is as follows:

AGI	Surtax rate	Combined tax rate
	Single returns	
Below $25,000	No surtax	14%
$25,000 to $37,500	12%	26%
Over $37,500	16%	30%
	Joint returns	
Below $40,000	No surtax	14%
$40,000 to $65,000	12%	26%
Over $65,000	16%	30%

For married persons filing separately, the tax brackets are half of the joint return tax brackets.

Corporate tax structure

The corporate income tax rate is set at a uniform 30% of taxable income thus eliminating graduation in corporate rates.

Base Broadening Measures
A. *Changes affecting individuals and unincorporated businesses:*
   1. The exclusions for income earned abroad by U.S. citizens, residents or government employees (secs. 911 and 912) are repealed.
   2. 7-year amortization for reforestation expenditures (sec. 194) is repealed.

3. 5-year amortization for pollution control facilities (sec. 169) is repealed.
4. Expensing of tertiary injectants (sec. 193) is repealed. Instead, these costs will be written off over 2 years.
5. A new depreciation method is provided for equipment and structures. Under the proposal, equipment is divided into 6 classes based on its ADR midpoint. An open ended account will be established for each asset class and each class will be given a class life. Each year taxpayers write off a percentage of the balance in the account, computed using the class life and the 250% declining balance method. Additions to each account will be made each year for purchases of assets in that class and subtractions will be made for dispositions of assets and for that year's depreciation deduction. Structures will be put into the sixth asset class. The asset classes and depreciation rates for equipment are as follows:

ADR Midpoint	Class life
Under 5	4
5.0 to 8.5	6
9.0 to 14.5	10
15 to 24	18
25 to 35	28
Over 35 and structures	40

For example, equipment with an ADR life of 10 years will be in the 10-year class. Thus, the first year's write-off will be 25% of the cost (2.5/10 = .25), the second year's write-off will be 18.75% (25% of 75%) and so forth.

This plan is designed so that the present value of depreciation deductions is approximately equal to the present value of economic depreciation at a 10% discount rate.

6. Percentage depletion (secs. 613 and 613A) and expensing of intangible drilling costs for oil, gas and geothermal wells (sec. 263(d)) are repealed. Instead,

there is a new system of capital cost recovery. Under this system, intangible drilling costs and those costs currently recovered through the depletion deduction will be written off under the same method applicable to equipment in the 10-year class. All costs incurred with respect to dry holes will be deducted when the well or property is abandoned.

7. Limits on qualified pension plans (sec. 415) are reduced from $30,000 on defined contribution plans and $90,000 on defined benefit plans to $15,000 and $45,000, respectively, and indexing of those limits is repealed.

8. The finance lease property rules (sec. 168(f)) are repealed and the pre-1981 law is restored.

9. The regular investment tax credit (sec. 46(a) (2) (B)) is repealed.

10. The research and development credit (sec. 44F) is repealed.

11. The credit for rehabilitation of buildings (sec. 46(a) (2) (F)) is repealed.

12. The business energy tax credits (secs. 46(a) (2) (c), 44D and 44E) are repealed.

13. All individual farms with gross receipts of more than $1 million and all farm syndicates will be required to use accrual accounting and to capitalize pre-production period expenses, and cannot use the expensing provisions for soil and water conservation expenditures (sec. 175), fertilizer (sec. 180), or land clearing (sec. 182).

14. Individuals with AGI above $100,000 would have to cover 90% of current year's tax liability with estimated or withheld tax payments.

15. Income averaging (sec. 1301) is repealed.

16. The child care credit (sec. 44A) is converted to a deduction for purposes of the base tax but not the surtax. The deduction is allowed to non-itemizers.

17. The political contribution tax credit (sec. 41) is repealed.

18. The exclusion of Tier II of Railroad Retirement benefits is repealed.

19. The exclusion for interest on cash value life insurance (sec. 804(a)) is repealed. Life insurance policyholders will include in gross income an amount equal to the increase in the cash surrender value of their policy during the year plus policyholder dividends received plus the "term insurance" value of insurance protection during the year minus the premiums paid. Insurance companies will provide policyholders with this information.

20. The exclusion for scholarship and fellowship income in excess of tuition (sec. 117) is repealed.

21. The deduction for second earners (sec. 221) is repealed because the new rate schedule sharply reduces the "marriage penalty."

22. The elderly tax credit (sec. 37) is repealed.

23. The general exclusions for interest and dividends (secs. 116 and 128) and the exclusion for reinvested public utility dividends (sec. 305(e)) are repealed.

24. Expensing of interest and taxes paid during the construction period of a building (sec. 189) is repealed and instead these costs are subject to a 10-year amortization.

25. The residential energy credit (sec. 44C) is repealed.

26. The deduction for 60% of net long-term capital gains (sec. 1202) is repealed and the distinction between short- and long-term capital gains is eliminated.

27. The individual minimum tax (sec. 55) is repealed. Since the legislation eliminates most of the preferences currently subject to the minimum tax, this provision is no longer needed.

28. The exclusion for unemployment compensation benefits (sec. 85) is repealed.

29. The exclusions for employer provided child care (sec. 129), education assistance (sec. 127) and group legal services (sec. 120) are repealed.

30. For purposes of computing the surtax (but not the base tax), a deduction would be allowed for all interest to the extent of investment income. For the base tax, itemized deductions would be allowed for all housing interest, and the itemized deduction for

other interest would be limited to investment income.

31. The exclusion for employer provided premiums on group term life insurance (sec. 79) is repealed.

32. The tax exemption for industrial development or housing bonds issued after December 31, 1984 (secs. 103(b) and 103A) is repealed.

33. Rapid amortization of low-income housing rehabilitation (sec. 167(k)) is repealed.

34. The itemized deduction for medical expenses (sec. 213) is limited to the excess over 10% of adjusted gross income.

35. The present exclusion for up to $125,000 of gain on the sale of a house by a person age 55 or over (sec. 121) is retained for the base tax but not the surtax.

36. The deduction for adoption expenses (sec. 222) is repealed.

37. The deduction for state and local income and real property taxes is retained but the deduction for all other state and local taxes (sec. 164) is repealed.

38. The exclusion for employer provided premiums on group health insurance (sec. 106) is repealed.

39. Indexing of the personal exemptions and the tax brackets (sec. 1(f)) is repealed because the new rate structure will greatly reduce the problem of "bracket creep."

40. Trusts and estates would be subject to a flat 30% tax on taxable income in excess of $100. As under present law, a deduction would be allowed for distributions.

B. *Changes affecting corporations:*

1. A new depreciation method is provided for equipment and structures. Under the proposal, equipment is divided into 6 classes based on its ADR midpoint. An open ended account will be established for each asset class and each class will be given a class life. Each year taxpayers write off a percentage of the balance in the account, computed using the class life and the 250% declining balance method. Additions

to each account will be made each year for purchases of assets in that class and subtractions will be made for dispositions of assets and for that year's depreciation deduction. Structures will be put into the sixth asset class. The asset classes and depreciation rates for equipment are as follows:

ADR Midpoint	Class life
Under 5	4
5.0 to 8.5	6
9.0 to 14.5	10
15 to 24	18
25 to 35	28
Over 35 and structures	40

For example, equipment with an ADR life of 10 years will be in the 10-year class. Thus, the first year's write-off will be 25% of the cost (2.5/10 = .25), the second year's write-off will be 18.75% (25% of 75%) and so forth.

This plan is designed so that the present value of depreciation deductions is approximately equal to the present value of economic depreciation at a 10% discount rate.

2. Percentage depletion for minerals (sec. 613) and expensing of mineral exploration and development costs (sec. 616 and 617) are repealed. Instead, there is a new system of capital cost recovery whereby exploration and development costs are deducted under an open account system based on 6 asset classes. These 6 classes are the same as those for equipment. Mines will be assigned to one of the 6 asset classes based on the expected useful life of the mine (using the same system that assigns equipment to each class based on its asset depreciation range (ADR) midpoint).

3. Percentage depletion (secs. 613 and 613A) and expensing of intangible drilling costs for oil, gas and geothermal wells (sec. 263(d)) are repealed. Instead,

there is a new system of capital cost recovery. Under this system, intangible drilling costs and those costs currently recovered through the depletion deduction will be written off under the same method applicable to equipment in the 10-year class. All costs incurred with respect to dry holes will be deducted when the well or property is abandoned.

4. The income of controlled foreign subsidiaries of U.S. corporations is subject to tax.

5. The preferential taxation of Domestic International Sales Corporations (DISC) (sec. 991) is repealed and previously deferred DISC income is recaptured over a 10-year period.

6. The deduction for bad debt reserves of financial institutions in excess of their actual experience (secs. 585 and 593) is repealed.

7. The exclusion for contributions to a maritime construction fund is repealed.

8. The finance lease property rules (sec. 168(f)) are repealed and the pre-1981 law is restored.

9. The regular investment tax credit (sec. 46(a) (2) (B)) is repealed.

10. The credit for possessions corporations (sec. 936) is repealed.

11. The research and development credit (sec. 44F) is repealed.

12. The credit for rehabilitation of buildings (sec. 46(a) (2) (F)) is repealed.

13. The business energy tax credits (secs. 46(a) (2) (c), 44D and 44E) are repealed.

14. The employer stock ownership credit (sec. 44G) is repealed.

15. For corporations, the deduction for charitable contributions is limited to one-half of such contributions. Thus they will receive a 15% tax benefit for charitable giving.

16. All corporate farms with gross receipts of more than $1 million and all farm syndicates will be required to use accrual accounting and to capitalize pre-produc-

tion period expenses, and cannot use the expensing provisions for soil and water conservation expenditures (sec. 175), fertilizer (sec. 180), or land clearing (sec. 182).

17. For taxpayers using the completed contract method, the 3-year exception is deleted and a "look-back" method, imposing interest charges on deferred tax liability, is implemented.

18. The alternative capital gains rate for corporations (sec. 1201) is repealed.

19. The exemption for credit unions (sec. 501(c) (14)) is repealed.

20. Expensing of magazine circulation expenditures (sec. 173) is repealed. Instead, these costs will be amortized over 10 years.

21. Expensing of tertiary injectants (sec. 193) is repealed. Instead, these costs will be written off over 2 years.

22. The exclusion of income attributable to a stock-for-debt swap (sec. 108) is repealed.

23. Upon liquidation, a corporation will recognize gain on all appreciated assets (secs. 336 and 337).

24. 7-year amortization for reforestation expenditures (sec. 194) is repealed.

25. 5-year amortization for pollution control facilities (sec. 169) is repealed.

26. Expensing of interest and taxes paid during the construction period of a building (sec. 189) is repealed and instead these costs are subject to a 10-year amortization.

27. The corporate minimum tax (sec. 56) is repealed. Since the legislation eliminates most of the preferences currently subject to the minimum tax, this provision is no longer needed.

28. The tax exemption for industrial development or housing bonds issued after December 31, 1984 (secs. 103(b) and 103A) is repealed.

29. Rapid amortization of low-income housing rehabilitation (sec. 167(k)) is repealed.

Single Taxpayer #1

	1984 Law	Proposal
Income: Salary	15,000	15,000
Plus: Employer paid health insurance	—	1,200
Employer paid life insurance	—	150
Equals: ADJUSTED GROSS INCOME	15,000	16,350
Less: Exemption	1,000	1,600
Equals: TAXABLE INCOME	14,000	14,750
TAX	1,801*	1,645**
Marginal tax rate	20%	14%

* From 1984 law tax rate tables

** Taxable income less $3,000 zero bracket amount times 14 percent tax rate

Married Taxpayer #1

	1984 Law	*Proposal*
Income: Salary	15,000*	15,000
Less: Two earner deduction	500	—
Plus: Employer paid life insurance	—	1,200
Employer paid health insurance	—	150
Equals: ADJUSTED GROSS INCOME	14,500	16,350
Less: Exemptions	4,000	5,200
Equals: TAXABLE INCOME	10,500	11,150
TAX	889**	721†
Marginal tax rate	14%	14%

---

* Assumed $10,000 earned by one spouse, $5,000 by other

** From 1984 law rate tables

† Taxable income less $6,000 zero bracket amount times 14 percent tax rate

Single Taxpayer #2

	1984 Law	Proposal
Income: Salary	30,000	30,000
Plus: Employer paid health insurance	—	1,200
Employer paid life insurance	—	300
Equals: ADJUSTED GROSS INCOME	30,000	31,500
Less: Exemption	1,000	1,600
Equals: TAXABLE INCOME	29,000	29,900
TAX	5,773*	4,546**
Marginal tax rate	34%	26%

---

* From 1984 law rate tables

** Taxable income less $3,000 zero bracket amount times 14 percent rate, plus surtax (12 percent of AGI over $25,000)

Married Taxpayer #2

	1984 Law	Proposal
Income: Salary	30,000*	30,000*
Less: Two earner deduction	1,000	—
Plus: Employer paid health insurance	—	1,200
Employer paid life insurance	—	300
Equals: ADJUSTED GROSS INCOME	29,000	31,500
Less: Exemptions	4,000	5,200
Child care deduction	—	2,000
Equals: TAXABLE INCOME	25,000	24,300
TAX BEFORE CREDIT	3,565**	2,562†
Less: Child care credit	400	—
Equals: TAX AFTER CREDIT	3,165	2,562
Marginal tax rate	25%	14%

---

* Assumed $20,000 earned by one spouse, $10,000 by the other
** From 1984 law rate tables
† Taxable income less $6,000 zero bracket amount times 14 percent tax rate

Single Taxpayer #3

	1984 Law	Proposal
Income: Salary	30,000	30,000
Plus: Employer paid health insurance	—	1,200
Employer paid life insurance	—	300
Equals: ADJUSTED GROSS INCOME	30,000	31,500
Itemized deductions:		
Mortgage interest	3,000	3,000
Property taxes	1,000	1,000
Sales taxes	250	—
Income taxes	1,200	1,200
Charitable contributions	500	500
TOTAL	5,950	5,700
Less: Zero bracket amount	2,300	3,000
Equals: EXCESS ITEMIZED DEDUCTIONS	3,650	2,700
AGI	30,000	31,500
Less: Exemptions	1,000	1,600
Less: Excess itemized deductions	3,650	2,700
Equals: TAXABLE INCOME	25,350	27,200
TAX	4,670*	4,168**
Marginal tax rate	30%	26%

* From 1984 law rate tables
** Taxable income less $3,000 zero bracket amount times 14 percent tax rate, plus surtax (12 percent of AGI over $25,000).

Married Taxpayer #3

	1984 Law	*Proposal*
Income: Salary	30,000*	30,000*
Less: Two earner deduction	1,000	—
Plus: Employer paid health insurance	—	1,200
Employer paid life insurance	—	300
Equals: ADJUSTED GROSS INCOME	29,000	31,500
Itemized deductions:		
Mortgage interest	3,000	3,000
Property taxes	1,000	1,000
Sales taxes	400	—
Income taxes	1,000	1,000
Charitable contributions	500	500
TOTAL	5,900	5,500
Less: Zero bracket amount	3,400	6,000
Equals: EXCESS ITEMIZED DEDUCTIONS	2,500	0
AGI	29,000	31,500
Less: Exemptions	4,000	5,200
Excess itemized deductions	2,500	0
Child care deduction	—	2,000
Equals: TAXABLE INCOME	22,500	24,300
TAX BEFORE CREDIT	3,003**	2,562†
Less: Child care credit	400	—
Equals: TAX AFTER CREDIT	2,603	2,562
Marginal tax rate	22%	14%

---

* Assumed $20,000 earned by one spouse, $10,000 by the other
** From 1984 law rate tables
† Taxable income less $6,000 zero bracket amount times 14 percent tax rate

Single Taxpayer #4

	1984 Law	Proposal
Income: Salary	60,000	60,000
Dividends	100	100
Less: Dividend exclusion	100	—
Plus: Employer paid health insurance	—	1,200
Employer paid life insurance	—	600
Equals: ADJUSTED GROSS INCOME	60,000	61,900
Itemized deductions:		
Mortgage interest	4,800	4,800
Property taxes	2,000	2,000
Sales taxes	700	—
Income taxes	3,000	3,000
Charitable contributions	1,500	1,500
TOTAL	12,000	11,300
Less: Zero bracket amount	2,300	3,000
Equals: EXCESS ITEMIZED DEDUCTIONS	9,700	8,300
AGI	60,000	61,900
Less: Exemption	1,000	1,600
Excess itemized deductions	9,700	8,300
Equals: TAXABLE INCOME	49,300	52,000
TAX	13,595*	12,264**
Marginal tax rate	45%	30%

---

* From 1984 law rate tables

** Taxable income less $3,000 zero bracket amount times 14 percent, plus surtax (12 percent of AGI from $25,000 to $37,500, and 16 percent of AGI in excess of $37,500).

Married Taxpayer #4

	1984 Law	Proposal
Income: Salary	60,000	60,000
Dividends	200	200
Less: Dividend exclusion	200	—
Two earner couple deduction	2,000	—
Plus: Employer paid health insurance	—	1,200
Employer paid life insurance	—	600
Equals: ADJUSTED GROSS INCOME	58,000	62,000
Itemized deductions:		
Mortgage interest	4,800	4,800
Property taxes	2,000	2,000
Sales taxes	800	—
Income taxes	2,400	2,400
Charitable contributions	1,500	1,500
TOTAL	11,500	10,700
Less: Zero bracket amount	3,400	6,000
Equals: EXCESS ITEMIZED DEDUCTIONS	8,100	4,700
AGI	58,000	62,000
Less: Exemptions	4,000	5,200
Excess itemized deductions	8,100	4,700
Child care deduction	—	3,000
Equals: TAXABLE INCOME	45,900	49,100
TAX BEFORE CREDIT	9,810*	8,674**
Less: Child care credit	600	—
Equals: TAX AFTER CREDIT	9,210	8,674
Marginal tax rate	38%	26%

---

* From 1984 law rate tables

** Taxable income less $6,000 zero bracket amount times 14 percent tax rate, plus surtax (12 percent of AGI over $40,000)

Single Taxpayer #5

	1984 Law	Proposal
Income: Salary	60,000	60,000
Long term capital gains	40,000	40,000
Interest and dividends	20,000	20,000
TOTAL	120,000	120,000
Less: Capital gain exclusion	24,000	—
Dividend exclusion	100	—
Plus: Employer paid health insurance	—	1,200
Employer paid life insurance	—	600
Equals: ADJUSTED GROSS INCOME	95,900	121,800
Itemized deductions:		
Mortgage interest	5,000	5,000
Other interest	5,000	5,000
Property tax	3,000	3,000
Sales tax	1,000	—
Income tax	7,500	7,500
Charitable contributions	5,000	5,000
TOTAL	26,500	25,500
Less: Zero bracket amount	2,300	3,000
Equals: EXCESS ITEMIZED DEDUCTIONS	24,200	22,500

	1984 Law	Proposal
AGI	95,900	121,800
Less: Exemption	1,000	1,600
Less: Excess itemized deductions	24,200	22,500
Equals: TAXABLE INCOME	70,700	97,700
TAX	23,507*	26,646**
Marginal tax rate: ordinary income	48%	30%
capital gains	19.2%	30%

---

* From 1984 law rate tables

** Taxable income less $3,000 zero bracket amount times 14 percent tax rate, plus surtax on AGI net of interest expense not in excess of investment income (12 percent from $25,000 to $37,500, and 16 percent over $37,500)

Married Taxpayer #5

	1984 Law	Proposal
Income: Salary	60,000*	60,000*
Long term capital gains	40,000	40,000
Interest and dividends	20,000	20,000
TOTAL	120,000	120,000
Less: Capital gain exclusion	24,000	—
Dividend exclusion	200	—
Two earner deduction	2,000	—
Plus: Employer paid health insurance	—	1,200
Employer paid life insurance	—	600
Equals: ADJUSTED GROSS INCOME	93,800	121,800
Itemized deductions:		
Mortgage interest	5,000	5,000
Other interest	5,000	5,000
Property tax	3,000	3,000
Sales tax	1,200	—
Income tax	7,000	7,000
Charitable contributions	5,000	5,000
TOTAL	26,200	25,000
Less: Zero bracket amount	3,400	6,000
Equals: EXCESS ITEMIZED DEDUCTION	22,800	19,000

	1984 Law	*Proposal*
AGI	93,800	121,800
Less: Exemptions	4,000	5,200
Excess itemized deductions	22,800	19,000
Child care deduction	—	4,000
Equals: TAXABLE INCOME	67,000	93,600
TAX BEFORE CREDIT	18,108**	22,752†
Less: Child care credit	800	—
TAX	17,308	22,752
Marginal tax rate: ordinary income	42%	30%
capital gains	16.8%	30%

---

* Assumed $40,000 earned by one spouse, $20,000 by the other

** From 1984 law rate tables

† Taxable income less $6,000 zero bracket amount times 14 percent tax rate, plus surtax on AGI net of interest expense not in excess of investment income (12 percent from $40,000 to $65,000, and 16 percent over $65,000)

Single Taxpayer #6

	1984 Law	Proposal
Income: Salary	60,000	60,000
Interest and dividends	60,000	60,000
TOTAL	120,000	120,000
Less: Dividend exclusion	100	—
Plus: Employer paid health insurance	—	1,200
Employer paid life insurance	—	600
Equals: ADJUSTED GROSS INCOME	119,900	121,800
Itemized deductions:		
Mortage interest	5,000	5,000
Other interest	5,000	5,000
Property tax	3,000	3,000
Sales tax	1,000	—
Income tax	7,500	7,500
Charitable contributions	5,000	5,000
TOTAL	26,500	25,500
Less: Zero bracket amount	2,300	3,000
Equals: EXCESS ITEMIZED DEDUCTIONS	24,200	22,500

	1984 Law	*Proposal*
AGI	119,900	121,800
Less: Exemption	1,000	1,600
Less: Excess itemized deductions	24,200	22,500
Equals: TAXABLE INCOME	94,700	97,700
TAX	35,285*	26,646**
Marginal tax rate: ordinary income	50%	30%
capital gains	20%	30%

---

* From 1984 law rate tables

** Taxable income less $3,000 zero bracket amount times 14 percent tax rate, plus surtax on AGI net of interest expense not in excess of investment income (12 percent from $25,000 to $37,500 and 16 percent over $37,500)

Married Taxpayer #6

	1984 Law	Proposal
Income: Salary	60,000*	60,000*
Interest and dividends	60,000	60,000
TOTAL	120,000	120,000
Less: Dividend exclusion	200	—
Two earner deduction	2,000	—
Plus: Employer paid health insurance	—	1,200
Employer paid life insurance	—	600
Equals: ADJUSTED GROSS INCOME	117,800	121,800
Itemized deductions:		
Mortgage interest	5,000	5,000
Other interest	5,000	5,000
Property tax	3,000	3,000
Sales tax	1,200	—
Income tax	7,000	7,000
Charitable contributions	5,000	5,000
TOTAL	26,200	25,000
Less: Zero bracket amount	3,400	6,000
Equals: EXCESS ITEMIZED DEDUCTION	22,800	19,000

Appendix

	1984 Law	Proposal
AGI	117,800	121,800
Less: Exemptions	4,000	5,200
Excess itemized deductions	22,800	19,000
Child care deduction	—	4,000
Equals: TAXABLE INCOME	91,000	93,600
TAX BEFORE CREDIT	28,350**	22,752†
Less: Child care credit	800	—
TAX	27,550	22,752
Marginal tax rate: ordinary income	45%	28%
capital gains	18%	28%

* Assumed $40,000 earned by one spouse, $20,000 by the other

** From 1984 law rate tables

† Taxable income less $6,000 zero bracket amount times 14 percent tax rate, plus surtax on AGI net of interest expense not in excess of investment income (12 percent from $40,000 to $65,000 and 16 percent over $65,000)

Married Taxpayer #7

	1984 Law	Proposal
Income: Salary	200,000*	200,000*
Long term capital gain	400,000	400,000
Interest and dividends	400,000	400,000
TOTAL	1,000,000	1,000,000
Less: Capital gain exclusion	240,000	—
Dividend exclusion	200	—
Two earner deduction	3,000	—
Plus: Employer paid health insurance	—	1,200
Employer paid life insurance	—	2,000
Equals: ADJUSTED GROSS INCOME	756,800	1,003,200
Itemized deductions:		
Mortgage interest	10,000	10,000
Other interest	100,000	100,000
Property tax	10,000	10,000
Sales tax	4,000	—
Income tax	100,000	100,000
Charitable contributions	50,000	50,000
TOTAL	274,000	270,000
Less: Zero bracket amount	3,400	6,000
Equals: EXCESS ITEMIZED DEDUCTIONS	270,600	264,000

	1984 Law	*Proposal*
AGI	756,800	1,003,200
Less: Exemptions	4,000	5,200
Excess itemized deductions	270,600	264,000
Child care deduction	—	4,800
Equals: TAXABLE INCOME	482,200	729,200
TAX BEFORE CREDIT	222,500**	236,760†
Less: Child care credit	960	—
TAX AFTER CREDIT	221,540	236,760
Marginal tax rate: Ordinary income	50%	30%
Capital gains	20%	30%

---

* Assumed at least $30,000 earned by lesser earning spouse

** From 1984 law rate tables

† Taxable income less $6,000 zero bracket amount times 14 percent tax rate, plus surtax on AGI net of interest expense not in excess of investment income (12 percent from $40,000 to $65,000 and 16 percent over $65,000)

Married Taxpayer #8

	1984 Law	Proposal
Income: Salary	200,000*	200,000*
Interest and dividends	800,000	800,000
TOTAL	1,000,000	1,000,000
Less: Dividend exclusion	200	—
Two earner deduction	3,000	—
Plus: Employer paid health insurance	—	1,200
Employer paid life insurance	—	2,000
Equals: ADJUSTED GROSS INCOME	996,800	1,003,200
Itemized deductions:		
Mortgage interest	10,000	10,000
Other interest	100,000	100,000
Property taxes	10,000	10,000
Sales taxes	4,000	—
Income taxes	100,000	100,000
Charitable contributions	50,000	50,000
TOTAL	274,150	270,000
Less: Zero bracket amount	3,400	6,000
Equals: EXCESS ITEMIZED DEDUCTIONS	270,600	264,000

	1984 Law	*Proposal*
AGI	996,800	1,003,200
Less: Exemptions	4,000	5,200
Excess itemized deductions	270,600	264,000
Child care deduction	—	4,800
Equals: TAXABLE INCOME	722,200	729,200
TAX BEFORE CREDIT	342,500**	236,760†
Less: Child care credit	960	—
TAX AFTER CREDIT	341,540	236,760
Marginal tax rate: Ordinary income	50%	30%
Capital gains	20%	30%

---

* Assumed at least $30,000 earned by lesser earning spouse

** From 1984 law rate tables

† Taxable income less $6,000 zero bracket amount times 14 percent tax rate, plus surtax on AGI net of interest expense not in excess of investment income (12 percent from $40,000 to $65,000 and 16 percent over $65,000)

Married Taxpayer #9

	1984 Law	Proposal
Income: Salary	200,000*	200,000*
Interest and dividends	800,000	800,000
Oil and gas partnership revenues	100,000	100,000
Less: Intangible drilling costs	1,000,000	142,857
Depletion	65,000	14,286
TOTAL	35,000	942,857
Less: Dividend exclusion	200	—
Two earner deduction	3,000	—
Plus: Employer paid health insurance	—	1,200
Employer paid life insurance	—	2,000
Equals: ADJUSTED GROSS INCOME	31,800	946,057
Itemized deductions:		
Mortgage interest	10,000	10,000
Other interest	100,000	100,000
Property taxes	10,000	10,000
Sales taxes	4,000	—
Income taxes	100,000	100,000
Charitable contributions	50,000	50,000
TOTAL	274,000	270,000
Less: Zero bracket amount	3,400	6,000
Equals: EXCESS ITEMIZED DEDUCTIONS	270,600	264,000

	1984 Law	*Proposal*
AGI	31,800	946,057
Less: Exemptions	4,000	5,200
Excess itemized deductions	270,600	264,000
Child care deduction	—	4,800
Equals: TAXABLE INCOME	–0–	672,057
TAX BEFORE CREDIT	–0–**	219,617†
Less: Child care credit	960	—
TAX AFTER CREDIT	–0–	219,617
MINIMUM TAX	158,000	—
TOTAL TAX	158,000	219,617
Marginal tax rate	20%	30%

---

* Assumes at least $30,000 earned by lesser earning spouse

** From 1984 law rate tables

† Taxable income less $6,000 zero bracket amount times 14 percent tax rate, plus surtax on AGI net of interest expense not in excess of investment income (12 percent from $40,000 to $65,000 and 16 percent over $65,000)

Married Taxpayer #10

	1984 Law	Proposal
Income: Salary	30,000*	30,000*
Less: Two earner deduction	1,000	—
Plus: Employer paid health insurance	—	1,200
Employer paid life insurance	—	300
Equals: ADJUSTED GROSS INCOME	29,000	31,500
Itemized deductions:		
Mortgage interest	5,000	5,000
Property taxes	1,500	1,500
Sales taxes	400	—
Income taxes	1,000	1,000
Charitable contributions	500	500
TOTAL	8,400	8,000
Less: Zero bracket amount	3,400	6,000
Equals: EXCESS ITEMIZED DEDUCTIONS	5,000	2,000
AGI	29,000	30,700
Less: Exemptions	4,000	5,000
Excess itemized deductions	5,000	2,000
Child care deduction	—	2,000
Equals: TAXABLE INCOME	20,000	22,300
TAX BEFORE CREDIT	2,461**	2,282†
Less: Child care credit	400	—
Equals: TAX AFTER CREDIT	2,061	2,282
Marginal tax rate	18%	14%

---

* Assumed $20,000 earned by one spouse, $10,000 by the other

** From 1984 law rate tables

† Taxable income less $6,000 zero bracket amount times 14 percent tax rate

190

A FAIR TAX NOW

TO:

President Ronald Reagan
House Speaker Thomas O'Neill
Senate Majority Leader Howard Baker

I'M FED UP. The present tax system is unfair. It's too complicated. And it doesn't help our country grow and prosper.

The current tax system lets some people pay no taxes at all while others, who make the same overall income and don't bury it in tax shelters, pay high tax rates. It takes armies of tax specialists to understand all of the complexities in the volumes of tax laws. Our economy can never thrive when people spend more time trying to figure out how to lose money just to avoid paying taxes rather than how to invest money where it will grow.

It doesn't have to be that way.

I want a tax system that's fair and simple enough for everyone to understand. I want a system that eliminates all the loopholes but leaves those deductions that are used by most people (such as home mortgage interest, taxes paid to state and local governments, charitable contributions). And I want a tax law that has lower rates but still requires those who make substantial incomes to pay more than those who are struggling to make ends meet.

That's why I support the Bradley-Gephardt FAIR TAX bill. I urge you to support it and see that it passes Congress and gets signed into law.

NAME   ADDRESS

_____

_____

_____

_____

_____

_____

_____

_____

_____

_____

Return to: Fair Tax Foundation, P.O. Box 76895, Washington, D.C. 20013